DNA OF TALENT

DISCOVERY · NURTURING · APPLICATION

KENE ILOENYOSI

Author of *Finding Your Sweet Spot*

DISCOVERY NURTURING APPLICATION

DNA

OF TALENT

A blueprint for discovering your talents and putting them to work

BOOKLOGIX*

Alpharetta, GA

ISBN: 978-1-61005-834-6
Library of Congress Control Number: 2016917827

10 9 8 7 6 5 4 3 2   1 0 2 4 1 6

Printed in the United States of America

⊗ This paper meets the requirements of ANSI/NISO Z39.48-1992 (Permanence of Paper)

Cover and text design by Lucy Iloenyosi, NeatWorks Inc.

Table of Contents

Acknowledgements

The more you learn, the more you realize how much there still is to learn. The process of writing this book, my second, has been a lesson in personal growth. Its development was truly a relay race, as I worked with three editors.

Amy Maclure, who worked with me on my first book, kicked off the first leg of this editing race. Amy, your feedback and the additional resources you recommended made the final product richer.

Monica Scheidt ran the second leg. Your edits made my language tighter and less wordy, and reading your comments has greatly improved my writing skills.

And when I thought the book was ready, along came Hani Stempler, who showed me that there was one final lap to run. You lunged into and attacked my manuscript like Zorro in a sword fight, and taught me so much about how to write in ways that keep the reader engaged. You really took me out of my head and into the reader's mind, and forced me to eliminate anything that could be a distraction to my readers.

This work is richer because of the three of you.

To my dear wife Lucy, your constant encouragement, questions, and push to think deeper and broader make me a better writer and speaker. Your creative genius has turned the manuscript into a book that is attractive to readers.

And most importantly, I give God the glory for this second book. You have given me the talents I use in writing and speaking, and the talented friends who have added immeasurably to this book.

SECTION ONE

THE CASE FOR TALENT

Why Average Is the Norm

Go to school, get good grades,
and you will become a success.
—*Conventional wisdom*

Sipola made good grades at school and had dreams of becoming an investment banker. She was thrilled to land a job at a real estate investment firm right out of college. She had achieved her dream sooner than she expected. Much to her disappointment, the excitement faded in less than five years. She loved the company she worked for, but the investment world was not what she thought it would be. She quit after six years and enrolled in cosmetology school. She had always had an interest in beauty and skin care, and thought this path would offer the fulfillment she desired. She completed cosmetology school in two years and decided to open a skin-care salon in an upscale Atlanta suburb. Sipola was happy about her new venture and poured her energies into it as her clientele grew steadily. She was good at this, and enjoyed what she did. Or so it seemed. Three years into running this new venture, she shut it down. Turns out she no longer found this career path fulfilling. Sipola's inner frustration grew, and she wanted answers to a deep, burning question: "How do I find a job I love and at which I can be very good?" That is a powerful question, and one which, statistics say, 75 percent of working adults, young and old, ask themselves every day in one way or another.

"How do you find a job you love and at which you can be very good or great?" The answer to this is the path to excellence and fulfillment in your career. In 2012, I published my first book, *Finding Your Sweet Spot*, and it launched my professional speaking career. As often as possible, I would take questions during or after my speech. I soon noticed a pattern in the questions. If you have not read my first book, let me give you the premise: your sweet spot is found at the intersection of your Talents, Interests, and Passion (or, your TIP). Most people understand what interests and passions are, but this thing called talent seems a bit nebulous. We seem to have a general idea about it but cannot put our finger on exactly what it is. Is it a skill? Something you enjoy doing? Something you do well? Or is it something for which you have a passion? There were so many questions on this topic that it was obvious: talent needed to be addressed alone and in depth.

This book will help you better understand the subject of talent. It may not make you an expert on the topic, but it will equip you with enough information to get you started on the journey to discovering your talent.

Though titled *DNA of Talent,* this book is not a study on the biology and science of talent. DNA stands for Discover, Nurture, and Apply, a simple expression of the phases we must go through if we want to use our talents in a fulfilling career. At some point, I will talk briefly about the biological nature of talent. I promise, it will be brief.

Our Workforce Today

Many organizations, and even countries, are operating below their potential because people don't fully understand the power and importance of utilizing their talents at work. The Gallup organization's 2015 employee engagement survey revealed that in the American workforce

- 50.8% were "Not Engaged" (work solely for a paycheck);
- 17.2% were "Actively Disengaged" (miserable at work);
- and only 32% were "Engaged" at work (love their work).

This study focused on the American workforce, but I suspect that the percentages above can also apply to the global workforce. If you add the less-developed countries where people are more focused on survival than fulfillment, the percentage of those engaged at work might end up much lower.

"So what's the big deal?" you might ask. The Gallup organization developed something called **"The Microeconomic Path Model."** This is a framework by which leaders and companies can maximize human nature to accelerate organizational performance.[1] It maps out the key factors that determine the success of any organization. They are:

1. Identify the strength of the employee.
2. Place the employee in the right role.
3. The employee works under great managers.
4. These lead to employee engagement (Engaged Employee) . . .
5. Which leads to engaged customers . . .
6. Which assures sustainable growth . . .
7. Leading to real profit increase (not one created by layoffs) . . .
8. Ultimately leading to stock or enterprise value increase.

The 2015 survey mentioned previously indicated that only 32% of the people in our workforce are in the Engaged category. Let that sink in for a minute. The success of every organization rests on about 32% of their workforce; the success of our economy rests on 32% of our workforce. If we look at the employee engagement survey results and the Microeconomic Path Model together, there are three possible assumptions we can make:

1. Only 32% of the people in the workforce discover their talents.
2. Only 32% of those who discover their talents are placed in the right role.
3. Only 32% of those who discover their talent and are placed in the right role end up with great managers.

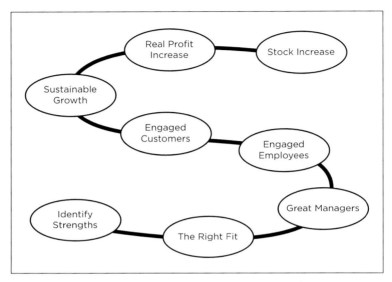

GALLUP Path Microeconomics: A behavioral economic model for organizations

I choose to believe the first assumption (only 32% of the people in the workforce discover their talents). Here's why: if you knew what you are really good at, you would be quicker to reject what you are not good at, and you would look for work roles and positions that use your talent.

Can this be true? Well, if the Pareto principle holds true (also known as the 80/20 rule), then yes, it is a good assumption. Some might be disappointed by this, but as an eternal optimist, I choose to see the upside. If the productivity and profitability we have seen to date have been achieved by the driving force of 32% of our workforce, what would become of our society if we increased the number of engaged employees to, say, 50% or even 60%? This should be seen as an important contributor to corporate and national success. Smart organizations (and nations) should be focused on creating an environment that facilitates real employee engagement, especially for the younger generations in the workforce. Millennials and Gen. Zs have been grossly misunderstood by older generations. Collectively, they are not lazy workers as many think. They are just motivated differently. They, like other generations before them, want the opportunity to do good work. Unlike other generations, however, they have a very low tolerance for work that does not engage them or align with their values. They want to love what they do, and will not be satisfied with working primarily for just a paycheck. If you are part of this younger generation, you know exactly what I mean.

So what is the key to engagement? Simple. Discover your talent, and figure out how to use it in a career you love. Unfortunately, most people do not achieve this goal because they are caught in what I call the Resume Trap. Some may even call it the Resume Curse.

The Resume Trap

A friend once complained to me that he was tired of changing jobs so many times and still not finding the fulfillment he craved.

"So, how do you look for new jobs?" I asked.

"I'm constantly updating my resume with my most current role and sending it to recruiters," he replied.

"That's the problem. You've been trapped by your resume," I responded.

He looked at me like I was speaking a foreign language.

The conventional human resource (HR) practice for hiring a new employee uses the applicant's resume to determine if they are fit for a role. If so, they are placed in the position. Hurrah!! HR has done their job. But have they really helped the organization? Is the individual really the right person for the job? Well, based on the resume, yes.

What is a resume? It is a chronicle of your past positions, roles, and accomplishments. In *Finding Your Sweet Spot*, I talked about the Skill Deception. If someone followed the traditional advice of "go to school, get good grades, and get a job," they most likely did not discover or develop their talent. They went and got a job after high school or college, and learned skills required for that job. Skills are great, but if you are not engaged in your talents with the right skills supporting them, you will burn out. The joy of a

Skills are great, but if you are not engaged in your talents with the right skills supporting them, you will burn out.

new job or position will fade quickly regardless of the perks that come with it. Those who never take the time to discover and develop their talents end up with a resume that chronicles their skills. HR looks at the resume (as they rightly should), makes a judgment based on the skills outlined in the resume, and matches the person to a job that requires that skill.

HR has done their part; the organization has filled a position, and the candidate has a job. The problem is that the corporation now has an employee who most likely does not have the talent for the key tasks performed in the position for which they were hired. This employee will end up in the "Not Engaged" category, and will never be able to give their best at work. Note, I did not say "do" their best; I said they will not "give" their best. Doing your best and giving your best are two different things. You can only give your best when you work in your area of strength or talent. When people work in their talent zone, amazing results are achieved. This is why the contribution of the 32% or the "Engaged" is what shapes organizations and ultimately our economy.

Young Professionals

Primarily, I work with young professionals, millennials (born between 1980 and 2000), so a lot of the examples and stories I use will speak to this demographic group. The goal is not to exclude, but to better serve my audience. That said, people in older and younger generations can learn a lot from reading this book. According to a 2016 PricewaterhouseCoopers global study, by the year 2020, millennials will make up fifty percent of the global workforce. Corporations are struggling to understand them and what makes them tick. The truth is that millennials, like generations before them, are also trying to understand themselves. They are the leaders of tomorrow. If they can discover and use their talents in work they love, I believe it will have a significant impact on the global economy. It will also shape how they raise their children, and help them discover and develop their talents much earlier in life. And I can help.

It is a very big dream, I admit, but why have small dreams? If you will dream, then by all means, dream big. My goal is to start a Talent Revolution and get as many people as possible using their talents to live a fulfilled life. My company focuses on developing resources and workshops to help adults and youth discover and develop their talents. Then, we figure out how to apply these talents toward a fruitful career.

I am inspired by the statement below from Johnson O'Connor,[2] one of my heroes in the Strengths movement.

"Many attempts to measure human beings have failed because they have treated the individual as a machine, dealt with him cold-bloodedly. They have arranged boys on an arbitrary intelligence scale running from zero at the bottom to one hundred at the top in such a way that everyone, except the one top individual, is discouraged, made to feel inferior to someone else. The application of science to the study of man must be inspiring, not disheartening; strengthening, not weakening. It must aim first to prove to each individual that he possesses a unique combination of abilities, one which the world has perhaps never seen before, and one which he can use to new purposes, to create new things, new thoughts. And having convinced him of his own strengths, it must then show him in what practical, concrete ways he can best use his particular combination of characteristics."[3]

—*Johnson O'Connor*

Choose to be different. Join me. Join the Talent Revolution; go to www.talentrevolution.me.

Enjoy the rest of the book.

CHAPTER ONE

Born This Way

Train up a child in the way they should go [and in keeping with their individual gift or bent], and when they are old they will not depart from it.

—Proverbs 22:6 (AMP)

Talent is an ability (aptitude) with which we are born. This is what I consider the best definition of talent. We are BORN with talent. Many people consider talent as something you are good at, or something you enjoy, or something for which you have a passion. All that can be true, as long as you were born with that something, and you developed it over time.

A Quick Overview of Talent

Talent Is an Ability or Set of Abilities with which One Is Born

Let us start with a biological view of talent; I will keep my promise to make this brief. Talent, this ability you possess, is really a neural path created in your brain while you were developing in the womb. The ability can be anything: how we think, speak, process information, organize information, handle objects, use our hands, relate to others, or even the shape or size of our body. Case in point is Olympics swimmer Michael Phelps. Many articles and documentaries have talked about his unusual arm-leg-torso ratio, which some speculate gives him an advantage in swimming. Phelps uses this to his advantage, and with extraordinary practice regimens, has developed himself into one of the greatest swimmers in the world. Every human being is born with certain neural paths (talents) already in place and developed to varying degrees.

This premise is most evident in children. If you take the time to observe children, you will notice that they are drawn to different things and behave differently from each other. Parents will attest to how certain traits can be observed in children as early as when they are a few months old. As the child gets older, one notices their affinity for or attention to certain activities. It is not unusual to see within the same family one child with a gentle personality and another with a rambunctious demeanor. Some children are outgoing, while others are reserved; some are deeply curious and inquisitive, while others display the general curiosity evidenced in most children.

Everything we do, say, or think starts in the brain. Most people do not develop their talents because parents may notice certain peculiarities about their children, but not focus on developing the particular trait in the child. As children grow into adults, these innate traits may unconsciously be taken for granted, especially if they are not related to music, sports, or theater.

If, however, the parents or the child identify certain traits and consciously work to develop them, the child makes significant progress in this trait rapidly by building muscle memory.

QUICK NOTE ON MUSCLE MEMORY:

While reading Daniel Coyle's book *The Talent Code,* I learned about "myelination." It simply refers to the process by which we build muscle memory. Myelin is a fatty substance that wraps around nerve fibers acting as a neural insulator, and serves to increase the speed of electrical communication between neurons (allowing our brain's messages to reach their destinations with greater speed and accuracy). With every repeated command our brain sends through our nerves, myelin grows and surrounds these particular circuits. The message literally sticks. When those commands are repeated often, the myelin surrounding those circuits increases, resulting in faster and stronger thoughts and movements. This process of myelin wrapping and increasing around the circuits is called myelination.

This is how we go from novices to experts; from conscious beginners to fluent experts in any activity. Myelination automates the activities we perform or in which we want to become proficient. Take driving a car for instance; when driving home from work or driving to a place you have been many times, are you consciously thinking about accelerating, slowing down, indicating, braking, turning, etc.? Most likely not; you are just driving. It's as if your body just knows what to do and when. This process is so ingrained that you could drive, talk on the phone, and eat a sandwich with ease and not lose control. Could you do this when you were learning to drive? Big fat NO!! When I was learning to drive, my mind was intensely focused on thinking about every process and action involved in driving, and I was exhausted after each driving session. Over time, I developed the muscle memory to perform the act of driving without thinking about driving.

This is why and how sports players can play their game without consciously thinking about the game, musicians play their instrument without thinking about where their hands should go next, or how we type without really thinking about where the keys are. Myelination is also how difficult subjects become easier for us as we practice them. It is all in the brain.

We Do Not Acquire Talent

As a child, Mike admired his surgeon dad. He loved to play doctor, and had dreams of becoming a surgeon just like Daddy. Frustration set in early when it dawned on Mike that he did not like biology or chemistry. He also noticed that during biology lab, he struggled with the proper handling of the tools used in class. Mike was not clumsy, but this just did not feel right. A disheartening thought crossed his mind one day:

"If I can't handle the tools now in biology lab, how will I operate on my patients in the future?"

Mike, and many of us, assume that we can be like our parents just because we are their kids. In some cases, yes we can. And in other cases, we cannot.

If we can't guarantee that we will be like our parents, how futile is it then trying to be like someone else? How often have we longed to do what someone else seems to do with ease? How often do we get jealous because we are not like someone else? This is especially prevalent in teenagers who, while still trying to assert their identity, may struggle with peer approval. Why would we want to be like someone else anyway? It's easy for me to ask this question now. As a teenager, I struggled with that self-identity and wanted to be like my friends, or brothers, or someone else. I saw them doing something that in some cases came naturally, and I wanted to do the same thing. By all means, emulate good behavior as much as possible; learn useful skills when you can, but accept that talent cannot be acquired.

Talent vs. Skill

Many people struggle with properly differentiating between skill and talent.

- **Talent:** A natural ability or aptitude, e.g., a talent for drawing.
- **Skill:** Expertise or ability derived from one's knowledge or practice. For example, learning to read or how to use a piece of software. A skill is something we are not born with, but which we learn. You might attend training to learn a skill like effective communication.

TALENT	SKILL
Nature: An ability we are born with	Nurture: An ability we learn
Signs are evident early	No visible evidence until it is learned
Faster development in the ability	Slower pace of development

What is a talent for one person may be a skill for another person. For example, there are people who find it easy to speak in public, and they enjoy it. They have a talent for communication. For many others, public speaking is a skill they have to learn. Glossophobia (the fear of speaking in public) has been ranked the number-one fear for years, with death ranked number-two. The majority of people, for whom public speaking does not come naturally, overcome this fear by learning and practicing the skills of effective communication. The person with the communication talent will most likely end up in a career that utilizes this talent most of the time, like as a professional speaker, emcee, news anchor, etc. And the person without the talent for public speaking, who develops communication as a skill, will never love or be energized by speaking in public; they will be satisfied with a job that may require that they speak in public every now and then. They will most likely never seek a professional speaking career.

Those of us who were born with the talent love to speak in public and are not afraid of it. However, the techniques of effective communication like speech organization, starting with an attention grabber, logical flow of ideas, using stories to make our points, etc., are all skills we must learn. The talented communicator loves to speak, but that does not make them a competent communicator. They become competent when they develop the skills that support the talent.

How Talents and Skills Work Together

Talents are supported by skills. We are born with talent; we acquire skills. What is a talent for one person may be an acquirable skill for another. The key question to ask is, "Will acquiring this skill help me in my talent zone?" If the answer is yes, then by all means go ahead and acquire the skill.

Many parents, unknowingly and unfortunately, gently coerce their children into a field in which they may not really have a talent. Instead, first figure out how our children are wired, then develop them along that bent. Having a certain pool of talents is no guarantee that your child will share the same exact talents. They may, but this is not a guarantee. The child may possess talents from a spouse or recessive abilities from previous generations. How often have you seen children who look more like a grandparent or great-grandparent than they do their parents? If this can happen with physical attributes, it can also happen with talents.

Focus first on discovering the talents you already have before you start trying to acquire skills that you may not really need. **STOP.** Go back and reread the advice from Johnson O'Connor at the end of the introductory chapter, on page 9.

If Not Used, Talent Is Not Lost—What is Lost Is the Opportunity to Effectively Use That Talent

There is the misconception that if you do not use your talents, they somehow disappear or fade away. That is not true. Such thinking comes from an incorrect interpretation of the Parable of The Talents in the Bible. In the parable, the King (who represents God) bestowed gifts (talents) on his servants. Some took those talents, used them, and multiplied them. They were faithful over what they were given and so reaped rewards aplenty. But one was afraid; he hid the Talents and did not use them. It lay dormant, so he did not reap the rewards from them. Here is an important lesson on making good use of our talents. It also applies to how we use other resources such as opportunities, money, and time. The talent itself was not lost; the one servant lost the opportunity to use what he had been given. But his abilities were not taken away.

Some people discover their talent in their later years. Depending on the talent, age and physical strength may be key factors in one's ability to perform a specific talent in a career. Those who discover or engage their talents later in life may end up using them only as a hobby or volunteer position. That is why I am on a mission to help young people discover their talents, because the younger you are, the better your chances of developing and using that talent in a fulfilling career the rest of your life.

The longer one waits to act on most talents, the shorter time one has to develop them. And this reduces the likelihood of achieving expert status in performance, or employment in a career.

MICHAEL JORDAN'S VENTURE INTO BASEBALL

In 1993, not too long after his father's death, Michael Jordan announced that he was retiring from the game of basketball. This came as a shock to his fans and the sports world, but not as big a shock as his 1994 signing of a contract to play minor league baseball with the Chicago White Sox. Turns out his dad always dreamt he would be a baseball player, and I guess Michael thought he could do it as well. After all, he had achieved great success on the basketball court and should be able to transfer the discipline to developing the skills required to play baseball professionally. Let's just say this did not work out as planned.

In March of 1995, Michael quit baseball and in the same month announced that he was going back to basketball. To understand why this happened, you have to go back to Michael's days in high school.

Michael Jordan was an athletic kid and played baseball, football, and basketball in high school. The story goes that he was not picked to play varsity basketball in his sophomore year because at 5 foot eleven, he was deemed too short to play at that level. Motivated to prove his worth, Jordan became the star of his high school's junior varsity squad. Coincidentally, he grew four inches by the next summer and finally earned a spot on the varsity team. Jordan remained active in basketball through high school, college, and the NBA. I have no doubt that he was still playing baseball, but it was not with the intensity with which he played and trained for basketball.

There was no way, having spent most of his active development years in basketball, that Michael would be able to play baseball at the level of those who had spent their active development years in baseball. He may have had the requisite talent to play baseball, but lost out on the years of development and practice needed to play in the major league. Time was no longer on his side. Now, if he had stuck with baseball from high school, would he most likely be celebrated today as one of the greatest baseball players ever? Who knows.

Some people are recognized for a talent later in life, and achieve something of surprising significance. They do not seem to have lost the opportunity to use their talents. That is correct. Why? They never stopped developing their talents; the recognition just came much later. Recognizing developed talent is different from developing the talent. We never lose our talents; we only lose the opportunity to use them if we never develop them.

Seek first to develop your talent, and in due time you may earn a Nobel Prize or at least "top dog" status at work.

Talent Is an Indicator of Your Life Purpose

"I don't know what to do with my life." If I had a dollar for the number of times I heard this, including the number of times I said it myself in the past, I would have a large vault of cash. Most people do not know what they want do with their lives. If we were to set up a booth for a week at Times Square in New York City, asking everyone who passed through (all 350,000 of them), I bet you that less than twenty percent would be able to tell you with certainty what they are meant to do with their lives. I also bet that those who are able to tell you what their life purpose is can also tell you what their strongest talents are.

In order to know why you are (one's purpose), you must first understand how you are. You can also throw in "who you are." We are human "beings" first, before human "doings." Understand "how you are" first and it will be easier to figure out "what to do." How you are is directly tied to what you should do career-wise.

What if Steve Jobs had become a pilot? What if Warren Buffett had become a geologist? What if Andrea Bocelli had continued as a lawyer? What if I had continued to devote my energies to the graphic design business and other ventures prior to that? The world would not have the iPhone, iPad, and other Apple products; a lot of people would not have become wealthy by investing in Berkshire Hathaway; lyrical Italian ballads would not have been written or heard; and I would not have written two books, or started Talent Revolution. These four individuals identified their strengths early in life and decided to pursue a life career that made use of how they are wired.

In this excerpt from a letter written by Albert Einstein to his college of choice, he makes his point perfectly:

> *If I am lucky and pass my exams, I will enroll in the Zurich Polytechnic. I will stay there four years to study Mathematics and Physics. I suppose I will become a teacher in these fields of science, opting for the theoretical part of these sciences.*

> *Here are the reasons that have led me to this plan. They are most of all, my personal talent for abstract thinking and mathematical thinking. My desires have also led me to the same decision. That is quite natural; everybody desires to do that for which he has a talent. Besides, I am attracted by the independence offered by the profession of science.[1]*

I once heard Warren Buffett say during one of his many joint interviews with Bill Gates that he is simply fortunate to live in a time where he could put his talent to maximum use. And if you are wondering what his talent is, my guess is a love of numbers combined with an ability to make sense of numbers.

Talent Is the Foundation of Living and Working in Your Sweet Spot

If your talent is not discovered, nurtured, and applied to the work you do or to your career, everything else will suffer. If you are not working in your talent, it is not a matter of "if" but a matter of "when" you will burn out. When you work in your talent zone, you operate out of who you are and how you naturally are. Outside of your talent zone, you operate out of the skills you have acquired.

For most people, their talents are naturally nourishing. I say "most" because there have been cases where a talent was abused in the development phase, and the person ended up attributing the abuse to the talent. That dilemma is not the topic of this book, but the situation can be remedied with the help of a good therapist or finding something for which the person has a passion, and to which they can use their talent. In *Finding Your Sweet Spot*, my main case study was Andre Agassi and his hatred for the game of tennis. He had the inherent ability to become an amazing tennis player, which he was. However, the rigorous (okay, ruthless) training regimen he was put through as a child caused him to develop a deep-seated disdain for the game that robbed him of his childhood. His attitude toward tennis did change later in life when he found a bigger purpose to live for: giving children from low-income families an opportunity to go to college . . . the very thing tennis robbed him of doing.

To recap, there are five things you should know about talent. They are:
1. Talent is an ability or set of abilities with which one is born.
2. We do not acquire talent.
3. If not used, talent is not lost. What is lost is the opportunity to effectively use the talent.
4. Talent is an indicator of your life purpose.
5. Talent is the foundation of living and working in your Sweet Spot.

CHAPTER TWO

The Talent Edge

Usain Bolt is currently the fastest runner in world with record times of 9.58 seconds for the 100-meter race and 19.14 seconds for the 200-meter race. I can beat Usain Bolt in a 200-meter race. Yes, you heard me correctly. I can beat Usain Bolt in a 200-meter race, IF he allows me a 180-meter head start. If I start running the race at the 180-meter mark, it will be tight, but I am certain that I will cross the finish line before Usain Bolt. You may be saying to yourself at this point, "Of course you will win the race, you were given a head start, and that gave you an unfair advantage." Working in your talent is like getting a 180-meter head start in a 200-meter race. That head start, that so-called unfair advantage, is the edge you have over others in your talent zone. This is the critical reason why you want to work in your talent zone.

Our talents give us three key advantages:

1. In our talent zone, we learn faster.
2. In our talent zone, we have greater capacity to do more.
3. In our talent zone, we are more intuitive, innovative, and creative.

In Our Talent Zone, We Learn Faster

A state department of transportation wanted to build a road connecting two neighboring cities. There already was a single-lane road connecting both cities, which had plenty of room for expansion on either side to create a two-to three-lane highway. The state agency had to consider other options to see if they could save money. Another option was to build a new route between the two cities that would cut through an existing forest. Imagine you were part of the decision-making panel; which option would you choose?

I bet you said the first option. The reason is obvious; there is already a connection between both cities, and all the state needs to do is expand it. Charting a new path would cost more as the DOT would first have to survey the land, map out the road path, probably buy the land if it is not government property, tear down trees, excavate roots and rocks, dig up the ground on which the new road would be laid, prepare the ground, and then start laying the road.

Remember the short explanation on myelination on page 13 of the previous chapter? Learning something requires creating new neural connections and/or strengthening those that already exist. Just as it is faster to expand the single-lane road into a multilane highway, strengthening neural connections and paths that already exist is faster than building new neural connections and paths.

This is why we say about some people, "They are a natural at . . ." and, "It comes so easily to them." The reason why people pick up or learn certain things faster than others is because of the preexistence of a neural connection. I am not saying you cannot learn something if the connection is not there, but the person with a preexisting connection will always have an edge. Always.

In 2013, I came across an organization called the Johnson O'Connor Research Foundation. They are a nonprofit organization dedicated to helping people discover their talents, and I was given an opportunity to participate in their comprehensive two-day testing program. On the first day, participants are put through a battery of tactile, visual, mental, and auditory tests over an eight-hour period. The second day is spent reviewing the results and their meaning with a test administrator.

During my review, my tester asked how many languages I speak. "I speak three languages fluently, and can make small talk in a number of languages," I answered. She had a look on her face that told me that there was more to her question. "Why do you ask?" I said.

"Well," she said, "you scored very high on our Silogram test."

"What test?" I replied.

"It's our test for measuring how fast you learn words, and you scored very high."

This was a big lightbulb moment for me. For as long as I can remember, I always had an interest in languages, but I had never really given it much thought or focus. I just thought it was an interest, like a hobby. I did not know I was born with the neural path in my brain. I have unconsciously used this ability so many times to my advantage without considering it a talent. In 2002, when I started in the moving industry, I had to learn Spanish quickly. I worked with teams made up predominantly of Hispanic guys, most of whom did not speak English very well. They had a great work ethic and I wanted them on my team. They were not aggressively learning to speak English, so I had to learn their language. If I did not learn it, our ineffective communication at work might have led to damages and injuries on the job. This was not an acceptable option. I bought a set of Spanish lessons on cassette tapes (yes, it was that long ago), and listened to them in my car on the drive to and from work. In about a month, I had learned enough functional Spanish to work with my team and hold a fairly decent conversation with them. Unfortunately, I stopped learning once we could communicate. I am not as fluent as I used to be, but I can still make small talk in Spanish. The same goes for a few other languages.

What things seem to come naturally to you? It may seem like an interest, or something you just do without giving it much thought.

_____

_____

_____

_____

Whatever it is that comes naturally to you, you will learn and develop faster than others in that same area.

In Our Talent Zone, We Have Greater Capacity to Do More

By virtue of the fact that we learn faster, and that our talents come naturally to us, it is easier for us to do more in our area of talent. There are people who are naturally gifted to work with numbers. Others are gifted to work with people, and others are gifted in working with systems and processes. When you work in an area in which you do not have a talent, it takes you longer to get things done; an hour feels like a whole day, and you feel drained of your energy at the end. For example, working with numbers: there are people who do not like working with numbers, but their job requires that they do. I can bet you they find no joy in this. The person who loves working with numbers will happily spend all their time working on spreadsheets. Put it this way, what the number lover can do in an hour may take the non-number lover two days to accomplish.

My wife owns a graphic design company, NeatWorks Inc., and for a number of years, we hired interns from the Art Institute of Atlanta for three-month terms, to give them the feel of a real work environment. Most went back to school at the end of the internship period, but every now and then, there would be one student who showed creative talent and who really wanted to learn more. They were offered a part-time position at the end of their internship. In 2007, Patrick came on as an intern. He was a hard worker, eager to learn, and really wanted to work with our company. My wife spent time teaching him different elements of design. One thing we always look for when hiring a designer is the raw talent and an eye for detail, both of which cannot really be taught, but can be developed (nurtured) over time if the talent is already there. Patrick did not have an eye for detail and he was slow in finishing his projects. His designs were average, not exceptional. We did not see that innate ability to intuitively match colors, images, and fonts in a balanced way. Patrick put in many long hours and tried to win a spot by working hard. We did not need a hard worker; we needed a really good designer. At the end of his three months, although Patrick was a hard worker, we could not hire him. The look of disappointment on his face hurt my wife and me, but it was the right thing to do.

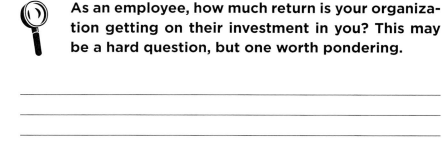

As an employee, how much return is your organization getting on their investment in you? This may be a hard question, but one worth pondering.

_____

_____

_____

_____

_____

About a month before Patrick started his internship with us, we had taken on Mark as an intern. Mark was not your typical hard worker. He came to work on time, took his lunch, and left right on time; he did not put in any extra hours. Mark, though, was a good designer with the intuitive abilities I just mentioned. He initially did not have an eye for detail, but caught on very quickly, unlike Patrick. What would take Patrick three hours to do, Mark would do in less than an hour and it would look much better. At the end of his internship, we hired Mark as a part-time employee. He never became a hard worker at our company, and he did not really need to. His designs were really good; he did a great job when he was at the office, was pleasant to work with, and was a great addition to the team. He was in his talent zone and, as such, had a greater capacity than Patrick. He did more in less time, and from a business standpoint, was a more valuable employee than Patrick. Every business wants a good return on investments, and this includes the investment they make in hiring an employee.

I told the story about Patrick at a conference in 2014, and a guy walked up to me later in the afternoon, saying, "I can't believe you did not hire Patrick. You made a wrong call." Let me be clear; I believe in working hard, but I first want to work smart before I work hard. Working in your talent zone is working smart. You will be amazed at what you can achieve in a short amount of time.

In Our Talent Zone, We Are More Intuitive, Innovative, and Creative

Imagination is more important than knowledge.
—Albert Einstein

John Maxwell said it best: "We are intuitive in our area of strength." A friend once asked my wife how she comes up with her design ideas. Lucy, my wife, did not know what to say. I have heard her say many times that she starts with a theme for the design, "and it just evolves from there." She cannot give you a formula or technique. I explain it this way: "The more you know, the easier it is to create from what you know." And trust me, every organization is crying out for new ideas at every level, ideas on how to generate more revenue or how to reduce overhead without affecting quality of service.

Do you remember when you started learning to ride a bike or drive a car? I bet you were a little bit—okay a lot—afraid. You were conscious of every movement, and your brain was very focused on riding or driving.

Now think again; do you remember when you stopped consciously thinking about riding or driving while riding or driving? I feel sure you can't. Somehow, you went from thinking about every action to driving without thinking (although the way some people drive makes one wonder what they are thinking).

In learning, we automate (encode) the process before we innovate (change) the process. According to Gordon Training International, we go through four phases when we engage in learning anything. The phases are:

1. Unconscious Incompetence: I do not know what I do not know.
2. Conscious Incompetence: I know what I do not know.
3. Conscious Competence: I am thinking while doing what I now know.
4. Unconscious Competence: I do what I know without thinking about it.

Source: Gordon Training International

Another way to look at the four phases is:

1. In Phase 1 – You are ignorant, even in your talent zone. You do not know anything.
2. In Phase 2 – You know you need to learn; this is the arousal/curiosity phase.
3. In Phase 3 – Learning really starts. This is where you start encoding the steps or processes required to do the task (driving, leading etc.). You initially start off thinking about every action, but this consciousness fades over time as you become more comfortable executing the task.
4. In Phase 4 – Your brain is on autopilot, operating more from muscle memory. The process is well encoded and your processing capacity is free to do other things. At this point it is easier to be creative.

No invention came out of thin air. Did Steve Jobs invent the phone, MP3 player, or the computer? No. He reinvented (through creativity and innovation) the phone, MP3 player, and computer into what we know today as the iPhone, iPod, and Mac; and he made Apple one of the most valuable companies today. He had a base of operating knowledge and talent that served as a springboard for his radical innovations. The best stockbrokers and fund managers have developed their market intuition over years, and are able to sense when to get in or get out of a market position. Warren Buffett has two simple rules to investing:

1. Never lose money.
2. Remember rule number one.

He has made some investment mistakes, but his talent and temperament have made him one of the greatest investors in the world. He knows a good opportunity when he sees one, and acts accordingly.

In your talent area, because you learn faster and have a greater capacity to do more, it gives you the advantage to come up with newer ways of doing things faster than those who do not share your talent. Companies today are starving for innovation and new ideas; they will not get it from employees who are not engaged because those workers are not using their talents; they are not really firing on all cylinders. Your "engaged" employees are the ones who come up with ideas on new products, revenue streams, process improvement, etc. In their area of strength, these workers see opportunities faster than others.

Your talent will always give you an edge over others without the same hard-wiring. The only time this will not hold true is when you put no effort into developing your talent. Talent never comes fully formed; you have to put in some sweat to develop it. I have seen many talented people who, for numerous reasons, failed to achieve their full potential. They did not work on their talent.

I once heard John Maxwell say that our strength can be our weakness when we fail to put in the work required to develop it. Raw talent on its own is average. And nobody will tolerate average for long. I am guilty of this sometimes. As a professional speaker, I never want to take it for granted that my talent in communication will always win the day. I must practice every speech thoroughly. I have had my fair share of squeaking by without giving my best to preparing for a speaking engagement. Even when the audience cannot tell, I know when I have not given my best. And it is not a satisfying feeling.

MEET CHEF AMY

Amy, a friend of ours, is an amazing chef. Yet she had no formal education in culinary arts, just a heavy dose of talent nurtured over the years watching her mother cook. Today, she is a private chef, serving an elite clientele. She has an intuitive sense for what ingredients go together and in what quantities. In February of 2014, Lucy and I came down with bad colds at the same time. Amy offered to come and make us some soup. I was quite disappointed when I saw the ingredients she laid out on the kitchen counter; kale, quinoa, carrots, celery, salt, and black pepper. As far as I was concerned, nothing delicious and exciting could come out of these things. How wrong I was. In the hands of an expert, simple things can be transformed into something extraordinary, and that was what Amy did. Like they say in the southern part of United States, the soup was "slap-your-mama-good." It was fit for a five-star dining experience. When I asked Amy for the recipe, she could not really remember the portions. It was made based on her intuition. A lot of her dishes evolve as they are being prepared. She just knows instinctively what to blend together.

Chapter Exercise

On a scale of 1 to 10, how productive are you at work (10 being extremely productive)?

_____

_____

Why did you give yourself the score above?

_____

_____

_____

_____

How productive would you be if you worked in your talent zone?

_____

_____

_____

_____

_____

_____

How productive would your team or organization be if most of employees worked in their talent zone?

_____

_____

_____

_____

_____

_____

CHAPTER THREE

You Don't Have to Be a Genius to Be Talented

It is not what you have that matters,
but what you do with what you have.
—*Unknown*

am often asked the question, "Are some people born geniuses?" The simple answer is, "Yes." But there is more to it than just being born a genius (or prodigy). Everyone is born with some talents, but not all of us are born geniuses. Geniuses are born with a much higher level of development (or neural pre-wiring) than others in a particular domain. I enjoy the study of geniuses, but most people are not born geniuses. So, this book is written for the majority of people who, like me, were/are born with average talent and who, through discovery and development, learn to use their talent in a fulfilling career doing something they love. Parents and teachers of geniuses and prodigies can learn a lot from this book, but it is not written for them. Sorry.

There are two levels of talent evident in children:

1. The Profoundly Talented: The geniuses or prodigies
2. The Moderately or Averagely Talented: The rest of us

The Profoundly Talented
(or Child Prodigies)

Child prodigies have been defined as "children under 10 years of age who perform culturally relevant tasks at a level that is rare even amongst highly trained professional adults in their field".[1] As those children display exceptional abilities at an extremely early age—an age that naturally limits the hours of training and practice that they could possibly have accumulated—innate talent must at least partly account for their early achievements.[2] One of the most famous prodigies is Wolfgang Amadeus Mozart who, according to anecdotal evidence, composed his first piece of music at age four.[3]

Key Characteristics of Child Prodigies

According to renowned professor of psychology Ellen Winner, in her book *Gifted Children: Myths and Realities,* gifted children (or what I term profoundly talented children) exhibit three characteristics:

1. They are highly precocious.
2. They are highly self-willed.
3. They have a rage to master.

These three attributes are echoed by many who have researched and written about highly gifted children. Let's look at these characteristics.

They Are Highly Precocious

A precocious child shows unusual advancement or development beyond their age in a particular domain/field. According to Winner, "They begin to take the first steps in the mastery of a particular domain at an earlier-than-average age. They also make more rapid progress in this domain than do ordinary children; because learning in this domain comes easily to them." (Remember myelination.)

ELON MUSK

What do the companies Tesla, PayPal, and SpaceX have in common? Elon Musk. He was the founder of PayPal, Tesla Motors, and SpaceX, the first private company to deliver a rocket that docked with the international space station to deliver supplies. Many people know about Elon Musk today, but few people know about the young Elon Musk.

He was born in South Africa in 1971 and grew up under the apartheid regime. As a child, he was very curious, read a lot, questioned everything, and showed a natural aptitude for entrepreneurship. He developed an early interest in computers, rockets, and space exploration. He was a nerd, and enjoyed making rockets and explosives. He was smaller and smarter than most of his age mates, and as such was bullied a lot. To escape the hurts of his childhood, he spent a lot of time programming and reading.

At the age of ten, he taught himself how to program and built a video game called *Blastar*. This video game was inspired by another popular video game called *Space Invaders*. He ended up selling *Blastar* to a magazine company for five hundred dollars. He was just twelve years old.[4]

They Are Highly Self-Willed

The self-willed have a strong insistence on marching to the beat of their own drummer. Winner puts it best. "Gifted children not only learn faster than average or even bright children but also learn in a qualitatively different way. They march to their own drummer: they need minimum help or scaffolding from adults in order to master their domain, and much of the time they teach themselves. The discoveries they make about their domain are exciting and motivating, and each leads the gifted child on to the next step. Often these children independently invent rules of the domain and devise novel, idiosyncratic ways of solving problems."[5] I could not agree with you more, Professor Winner.

MEET JOEY ALEXANDER

Joey who? That's exactly what I said when I saw the story on *60 Minutes* in early 2016. Joey Alexander is a two-time Grammy Award nominee. He released a jazz album (which earned him the nominations), and was working on his second album at the time of this writing. He has performed at the Newport Jazz Festival, an exclusive festival where artists have to be invited to perform; many famous jazz artists have not been invited, and Joey is currently the youngest person ever invited to play on that stage. Joey is just twelve. Hearing this, you would expect him to be from a rich jazz pedigree and born in a jazz-saturated culture in the United States. Joey was born in Bali, a tiny Indonesian island known more for its tourist appeal than jazz.

At his young age, Joey has already developed his own style of jazz, improvising like someone who has been playing for decades. As a child, Joey's parents said he was bursting with energy, and at the age of six he was given a keyboard as an outlet for his energy. I do not know why his parents chose music and not sports, but I sense they may have noticed some affinity with music. This is yet to be determined. Joey learned to play music by listening to his dad's collections of some of the jazz greats like Duke Ellington and Charlie Parker.

On the TV program *60 Minutes*, Anderson Cooper asked Gary Walker, music director at jazz radio station WBGO, "Is he good for a twelve-year-old? Or is he just good?"

"He's just good," Walker said. "At any age, his language is pretty special. But at the age of twelve, you almost think, you know, I might even believe in reincarnation, perhaps."[6]

They Have a Rage to Master

Highly gifted children have a predisposition or internal drive to learn more or understand the field for which they have a gift. This drive to learn borders on obsession, and it is marked by an intense interest and an ability to focus—like laser-sharp focus—on their involvement in this domain. This is what they want to do, and all they want to do. When engaged in this, they lose all sense of time. It is like the more they know, the more they want to know. The better they become, the better they want to become. This obsession, paired with the ability to learn it, leads to rapid growth and very high achievement.

THE TEN-YEAR-OLD COLLEGE GRADUATE

Michael Kearney, born in 1982, is the holder of four world records (for early enrollment in and graduation from school) in the Guinness Book of World Records. He began to speak at the age of four months. When he was six months old, his mother took him to a pediatrician with an ear infection. When the pediatrician said, "Now, Mrs. Kearney, what seems to be Michael's problem?" Michael said, "I have a left-ear infection." At the age of three, he discovered and proved the commutative, associative, and identity rules in algebra, announcing gleefully, "Dad, what could be more fun than math!" When his dad came home from work each day, Michael would greet his father with, "Dad, let's go do work," then insistently pulled his dad toward some math books. "Michael has a raging desire to learn," his father said. His parents say they actually tried to slow him down, but nothing could stop him. When he was interested in something, his concentration was intense.

At five, Michael entered high school, completing it nine months later. At the age of six, he then enrolled at San Joaquin Junior College, where he majored in geology. At eight, he transferred to the University of South Alabama, where he graduated fourteen months later at the age of ten, with a 3.6 grade point average and a degree in anthropology. After taking eighteen months off, he enrolled at Middle Tennessee State University, graduating with an MS in chemistry in August 1998 at the age of fourteen.[7]

Before you get sad about you or your child not being profoundly talented, let me reassure you that this in no way limits anyone's ability to succeed. Possession of profound talent is no guarantee of future success. Records have shown that many children who start out profoundly gifted end up as average adults who, although they still possess talent, end up not utilizing it to its full potential. Most people fall into the second category: averagely talented.

Averagely Talented

Most of us are in this category. This group can be sliced further into subgroups of very bright children all the way to your normal, everyday child who does not naturally excel in a field but still possesses talent. Those at the top of this group may have prodigy traits like being precocious, but lack the rage to master and/or the self-will evident in profoundly talented kids. Where you start out does not matter; what you do with your talent is the important thing.

I study and teach on the topic of talent, so I can make the next statement with confidence. Talent is important, but it is just the first step. Having talent means nothing if you do not do the work to develop and use it. I have a childhood friend who was gifted in math. He was always at the top of his class through high school. When he got into college, he got carried away with having a social life and stopped taking his studies seriously. He got kicked out of that school and transferred to a different one. Things did not get better as he refused to study and take school seriously. I am not sure if he ever graduated.

> *The choices we make in the development and application of our talent are far more important than the talents on their own.*

The choices we make in the development and application of our talent are far more important than the talents on their own. I love what Will Smith said: "I have always considered myself to be just average in talent. But what I have is a ridiculous insane obsessiveness for practice and preparation."

I do not know what percentage of the world's population is genius, and I really do not care. I want to focus on the discovery and development of the talents in as many people as possible.

In the biblical Parable of the Talents, it is interesting to really understand the King's reaction to the man who returned his one talent, telling the King that he had not done anything with it.

The master was furious. "That is a terrible way to live! It is criminal to live cautiously like that! If you knew I was after the best, **why did you do less than the least?** The least you could have done would have been to invest the sum with the bankers, where at least I would have gotten a little interest. Take the thousand and give it to the one who risked the most. And get rid of this 'play-it-safe' who will not go out on a limb." Matthew 25:26–30 [The Message Version], emphasis: the author)

Read the emphasized question again: **"Why did you do less than the least?"** I believe the King was more interested in the talent being put to use than it being returned to Him. The bigger lesson here is that it is more important to use your average talent than it is to sulk about not being as gifted as geniuses.

For talent to be of value, it must go through the DNA phases: Discovery, Nurture, and Application. The rest of this book will focus on these three critical phases.

Reflect on Section 1

What key lessons have you learned in this section?

_____

_____

_____

_____

_____

_____

_____

_____

_____

_____

_____

_____

Why is it important for you to discover your talents?

_____

_____

_____

_____

_____

_____

_____

_____

_____

_____

_____

_____

THE DNA PROCESS

CHAPTER FOUR

Discover Your Talent

n 1994, I got to spend a year with my uncle Al who is a lapidarist (an expert in precious stones and the art or techniques used in cutting and engraving them), and I got to learn a bit about precious stones and the people who mine them. The first time I watched him purchase raw stones turned out to be a huge lesson applicable today to talent discovery.

Uncle Al was well known by the local miners, and he was their first go-to buyer. Prior to my first stone-buying experience, all the stones I saw were well cut and polished, pretty much ready for sale. So I was quite disappointed when I saw the dirty rocks produced by the first set of sellers. Uncle Al saw the look on my face and smiled. He knew what I was thinking and so did the stone sellers; the kid from the city is looking for the shiny stones. Uncle Al proceeded to examine each dirty rock with his eyepiece on. He also had a small tool that looked like a cross between a hammer and a pickaxe, and with this he would gently chip away at different parts of the rock in his hand till he got to something that satisfied him. Then he would set it down in a to-buy pile. I was looking at the to-buy pile, and still, all I could see were dirty-looking colored stones.

These dirty-looking colored stones were the source of income for these miners, my uncle Al, and the many jewelers around the world who are far removed from this early process. At the end of the sale process, I asked Uncle Al how the miners know what to look for and where to get the best stones. His answer is more profound to me today than it was then. "They do not go in looking for the best stones; they just go digging for stones. And some days they are lucky to dig up something of immense value, but that is not the norm. The stones have been in the earth since the beginning of time and we did not put them there; the miners do not control the quality of what they find; they take what they **discover** and we make the best we can of it."

Just like we do not have a say in what minerals are found in the ground, we also do not have a say in the talents with which we are born. Our job, like my Uncle Al said, is "to take what we discover and make the

We are all born with certain talents; our job is to first discover them.

best of it." And like the miners who start each work day knowing there are precious stones in the ground waiting to be discovered, we must also start our search for talent with the mindset that there is treasure in us, and our job is to discover it and make the best use of it.

Unfortunately, most people do not discover their talents, and end up working their whole lives in jobs and careers that are not fulfilling. All they have to look forward to is retirement. If you spend all your life in unfulfilling jobs and careers, you will spend your retirement in regret for not pushing to live a more fulfilled work life.

If you are a college student or young professional, make the commitment now to discover your talents, develop them (through school or at work), and then get a job or start a business where you can use your talent to add immense value to your company or clients, and live a fulfilling life. This is what I call a "talent-based and purpose-driven" life.

To discover our talents, we must revisit our childhood. This is the period when our natural pre-wiring is on display. In spite of this, talents are often not discovered early in averagely talented kids because our parents and teachers have not been taught how to discover these talents. It is much easier to put a finger on talent in profoundly gifted kids. However, with some insight and understanding, you can become a **"Talent Miner,"** and discover your talents and the talents of your children.

Talent Miner: I use this term to describe a person who intentionally observes themselves. If they are parents or teachers, they also do this for children in their care.

Three Keys to Discovering Your Talent

1. Understand the age 1–10 window.
2. Average is where we all start.
3. Intentional observation makes the difference.

These three keys apply whether you are working to discover your talents or those of your kids. Let us look at each one individually.

Understand the Age 1–10 Window

Some children like to color, with Mom's lipstick. And some like to take apart every electronic item they get their hands on. Some are always trying to help others, and others are always the boss. The list is endless.

I refer to this age 1–10 period as the age of innocence; kids are just being kids, or so we think. Remember, we were born with certain neural connections in place. These neural connections determine what we like or do not like, how we respond to certain stimuli, what activities engage our undivided attention, etc. There are things we did as children that were not taught to us; we simply expressed who and how we are naturally wired to the world around us. Anything you did, or trait you exhibited consistently, as a child can be an indicator of what your talents are. Albert Einstein and Isaac Newton were very curious kids. Curiosity is what leads to new ideas and inventions.

Why We Miss the Sparks of Talent

When we were kids, many of the adults in our lives were more focused on preparing us for a career than they were in understanding who we are and what talents we were born with. This was not on their radar because they may not have known much about talent and how it manifests in most children. Sadly, when talent is discussed in children, it is ascribed more to the domain of sports, music, chess, math, and a few other categories. The discussion is more focused on the prodigies who start off naturally at a performance level that is advanced beyond their age.

The problem then for most of us is that what we did well as children may not have manifested in activities and performance levels that caused people to take special notice. The sparks of talent for most people in the age 1–10 phase show up in how they play, how they relate to people or things, certain patterns of behavior (like being chatty), which some may even find irritating, etc. It may even manifest in the games we liked to play as a child. I know a six-year-old child who, from the time he was two years old, loved the outdoors. I am not talking about just being outside; he loves trees, bushes, and flowers. It is not unusual to see him just standing on his own, next to a bush or tree in a neighbor's yard. Why is he like that? I don't know. It's just the way he is. The bigger question is, "Will this trait be nurtured by the parents?"

In my speeches and workshops, I often use the example of kids who throw a fit when food served on their plate touches each other. If you are or were like this, you are probably squirming right now. It is okay; I get the same look from those in the audience who have this trait. And I ask them to put up their hands. I then ask, of those whose hands are up, how many of them would say they are very organized in many or most areas of their lives. Every time I conduct this experiment, EVERY TIME, 80–100 percent of the people who do not like their food touching on a plate also say they are organized in many or most areas of their lives. In some sessions, some attendees have admitted that their friends have often labeled them as being very particular or even obsessive about order in their space.

What does this mean? Simple. The child who throws a fit because foods touching on the plate are about to enter their mouths is really a child pre-wired for order. Their inborn wiring for order is unconsciously kicking against the seeming disorder on the plate, and made worse because it is about to invade their internal space. They feel the same way you would if someone tried to feed you a live bug. Unfortunately, most parents, ignorant of these sparks of talent, tell them the same thing: "Eat it; it's all going to the same place." I bet your mom told you that. Or wait, maybe you've told your child that a number of times.

For children, play is their work. And children play most times based on how they are wired. As we become adults, we should not stop playing but should develop our natural way of play into something that we can put to work. This way, as adults we keep playing at work, but now we get paid to play, and our play (work) serves a useful purpose to our organization. As you start to revisit your own age 1–10 phase of life, I want you to also become more attuned to what and how your children play.

Fulfilling work happens when an adult works in their talent zone; they are now paid to play.

Average Is Where We All Start

I once heard John Maxwell tell this story to make a point. Some tourists travelling through a small, European village stopped to take in the scenery. The village had nice little cottages, cobblestone roads, beautiful waterways coursing through, and it was surrounded by lush, rolling hills. It was picture perfect. The tourists were so taken by the beauty of the village and wondered if any famous person had been born there. They decided to investigate, and came upon an old man sitting in front of a cottage in a rocking chair. This old man looked like he had lived there all his life. They approached him, introduced themselves, and asked, "Sir, we are so taken by the beauty of this village and how all the original features have been maintained. We wanted to know, was any great man or woman born in this village?" Rocking back and forth in his chair, the old man rubbed his chin and thought for a moment and then replied, "Nope, only babies."

No one is born great; we are all born, and become great, based on what we do with our lives. When it comes to talent, we all start out average. We were all born average children. I know your parents told you that you were born excellent. You were not. They had to tell you that; it is what parents tell their kids, and I will tell my kids the same thing. But the truth is, we are all born average. Even the so-called geniuses are born average. Even though they start out way ahead of most people and exhibit a higher level of giftedness, they don't start making significant contributions to this domain till after years of development and training. The earliest indication may be in their teenage years. Mozart was composing music by age six, but what many consider his first masterpiece, Piano Concerto no. 9 was written at age twenty-one.

Excellence is a by-product of development and mastery of a certain domain to the extent that you are able to make a significant contribution to this domain or completely alter it. I have yet to hear of a child who has achieved this.

> **All children are born average, but the difference is that we are born uniquely average . . . Born average, but unique and different.**

All children are born average, but the difference is that we are born **uniquely average**. Your unique average is different from my unique average, and different from the unique average of every other person out there. *Born average, but unique and different.* The key is to work our unique average talent and develop it into excellent talent with which we can live significant and fulfilling lives. We will talk more about this in the section on nurturing.

When I work with people in the talent discovery phase, I often hear them say, "Well I was not good at anything as a child." And as we dig deeper and start uncovering some average unique things they did as children, they all say the same thing: "That cannot be a talent; everyone one is like that." Or they say, "Oh, that is just the way I am. There is nothing to that." Sorry, everyone is not like that, and there is something to the way you are.

Janet, a client of mine, had spent years in the defense and security sector and was never fulfilled in what she did. She was in her fifties and desperately wanted to make a change. As we delved into her age 1–10 phase, she talked about how she was always helping people, and was very fond of the elderly. It was obvious that she did not know how her face lit up when she talked about this; the little child came out. The child in us never goes away; we just learn how to be big kids. I stopped her and asked why she did not see helping people as a talent. "That is not a talent, Kene; everybody should enjoy helping people." Wrong. I think we should all be helpful, but not everyone is naturally wired like that. It is like a gift of mercy or compassion; some have it and many people do not. Those who do not have it will learn to be compassionate, but it will not drive their lives.

Janet was looking for what she thought were big things, like leading people or being a math whiz. I have not read Mother Teresa's biography, but I suspect that some things in her childhood would point to her capacity for compassion. We start out average, develop our average, and then figure out how to use what we have. Janet then mentioned that for many years, she had led groups visiting nursing homes, taking meals to the residents and just spending time talking with them. She really enjoyed doing that. I asked why she had never considered working at a nursing home or retirement home. The look on her face was like she had seen a unicorn. She never considered this because she did not see this as a talent that would set her apart in this industry. With the new way of thinking, she has started considering how she might work in the elder-care industry.

You were born average, but uniquely average. It is not what you were born with that matters, but what you do with it.

Intentional Observation Makes the Difference

I call this "intentional" observation because I want readers to understand that it takes some effort to figure this talent thing out. It is not casual observation, but observation driven by and with intent, belief, passion, and focus.

Think back to the miners who sold their stones to Uncle Al. These guys did not have fancy tools or fancy mining operations. They were mostly uneducated people who mined on large tracts of land that had been in their family for generations. The land had been used for subsistence farming before the discovery of precious stones. I do not know who discovered the first stones, but judging from the size of the large holes in the ground, they had been mining for years. Their fathers and grandfathers mined the land, and these men intend to pass the land on to their children.

Why is this short story important? Think about it. Why have they kept these large parcels of land in the family? Why do they get up each day to work in their small mines? Because they know that there is treasure in the ground. They wake up each day with the mindset that there is something to be discovered, and they dig meticulously every day. As they dig, their eyes are not just casually glancing at the rocks they unearth, but are intently looking for little signs that may reveal a worthy stone. To the untrained eye, these men are just digging in the dirt. But the trained eyes of those digging are able to tell treasure apart from dirt. I am sure they do not find stones of value every day, but they keep digging. They are intentional about their work.

To discover your talent, you have to be intentional about observing and exploring your life. You do not start the process and give up after a week. You keep exploring till you discover the treasures that lie within you.

The greatest discovery in life is self-discovery.
Until you find yourself you will always be someone else.
—Myles Munroe

The observation process is not easy, but it becomes fun after a while. You start evaluating the things you did as a child against some of the things you do today. Self-discovery is quite interesting; you become a kind of student of yourself, and really learn things about who you are. I love it when a client or member of the audience has an "aha moment," and they catch a glimpse of something in their childhood that seems to explain a number of things they do today. The successful observer must keep a journal or an app on their smartphone handy in order to jot down observations immediately. The more you learn to observe and understand yourself, you just may find that it is easier for you to observe and understand others as well.

I must also warn that you may discover things about yourself that are not pleasant, things that bring up painful memories or feelings. If this happens, it is okay to take a break and seek a professional therapist if you need to, but please do not avoid the process. I once worked with a lady who liked to draw and color as a child, but was always told her drawings were no good and that she should quit. She took a different career path. When digging into her childhood, you could tell that there were some raw emotions that came with reconnecting to her talent. She remembered how much she enjoyed art as a child, and also the hurt of not being affirmed.

Many adults are empty and unfulfilled in their work, not because they lack talent, but because nobody helped them discover and utilize their talent. This may be your story. If you have come this far, it is because you know there is talent in you and you are ready to start digging. So, DIG.

Chapter Exercise

NOTE: This process may take a few days to a few months. You are worth the time required to discover this treasure.

In the exercise below, list what you see as your talents. Do not worry about trying to fit into a label, just describe your answers in response to the questions. You can use a single sentence or a word. It may help to talk with your parents and siblings, if possible, to fill in gaps. Childhood friends may trigger some memories as well. Get a notepad or journal; you'll want to document your observations.

AGE 1–10

What do you remember doing well as a child? What did you enjoy spending time doing most of all? List everything that comes to mind, and then think through each one. Talk with parents or siblings. Examples:
- **I was very curious about how things worked.**
- **I liked taking things apart.**
- **I liked to cook and play pretend chef.**

_____

_____

_____

_____

_____

_____

_____

_____

_____

_____

_____

_____

_____

_____

Do you see any patterns in some of the things listed? Example: you liked to dabble with color and you liked to draw. Or, you were always selling something—lemonade, Girl Scout cookies, stamps, or your own toys. Group the similar observations together (if any).

_____

_____

_____

_____

_____

_____

_____

_____

_____

_____

_____

YOUR TODAY

From the patterns you have described above, are there any traits you employ today, or that your friends and family say that you utilize? Maybe you are very organized, and you are still the one who likes to research and plan family events and vacations.

_____

_____

_____

_____

_____

_____

_____

_____

_____

_____

_____

Are there things people tell you that you do well today, and your response is, "It's nothing special; it's just something I do"? If there is, know that you "just do it" because it comes naturally to you. Do not take it for granted.

_____

_____

_____

_____

_____

_____

_____

_____

_____

_____

_____

Are there some traits/abilities listed that you use at work, at school, or in the pursuit of a hobby today?

_____

_____

_____

_____

_____

_____

_____

_____

_____

_____

_____

_____

_____

_____

CHAPTER FIVE

Nurture Your Talent

L iving a talent-based life starts with discovering your talent, but it is just the first step, not the difference maker. My Uncle Al would buy a small bag of raw stones that maybe weighed close to 4 lbs. (1.8 kg). He would then spend about three or four months cutting, grinding, sanding, and polishing the final products to be sold. The process was very tedious and meticulous as you can imagine, and most days, he would work late into the night. By the time the stones were ready for sale, the rocks that weighed about 4 lbs. had been reduced to a total weight of less than 1 lb. And here's the kicker: the dirty raw stones were purchased for a total of close to five hundred dollars, but the finished cut, polished, and sparkling stones would be sold for twenty to thirty thousand dollars. That's the power of nurturing your talent.

If you don't develop your talent from average to excellent, you will still end up not being fulfilled at work and in life. Nurturing your talent is what determines what you will make of it in life. This is where the grind happens, where the rubber meets the proverbial road. Sadly, this is where people start to jump ship.

BACK TO SIPOLA'S STORY

Do you remember my friend Sipola from the introductory chapter? She was one of the first people to read my first book, *Finding Your Sweet Spot*, and she had tons of questions when she was done. As we explored her life, a recurring trait that we noticed was how she was always looking for ways to improve how things are done. From simple everyday tasks like how she does her grocery shopping or how they run their home, to helping her friends think through the process of starting or improving their small business. Seeing inefficiencies in a system or process seemed so second nature to her; she never considered it a valuable and marketable work trait. In a conversation with my wife, she said of her skin-care business, "It's weird, but what I enjoyed most about my business was setting it up and putting all the processes and procedures in place, and seeing that it worked. Once that was done, I just got bored."

As we talked about this trait, the question she kept asking was, "How can I use this at work?" I knew she was struggling to see the immense value of her talent. Once she embraced this way of thinking as a talent, her next step was to figure out what to do with it. Well, for one, she needed to develop this trait. The Kaizen method, made famous by Toyota in Japan and introduced to the Western world in 1986, has led to a growing demand for process improvement experts in the workplace. My friend, having no formal training in this area, decided to get an MBA; but she did not stop there. She started offering to help small businesses and small nonprofit organizations with process improvement. She had figured out her talent, and knew that it had value, but it was still far from a marketable value to a large organization; she had to nurture her talent.

The 10,000 Hour Rule—Simplified

Nurturing talent is hard work, and it takes time. K. Anders Ericsson, known for his research in the field of expertise development, put forth the theory that it takes about ten years or ten thousand hours of deliberate practice to transform average talent into world-class talent.[1] It takes time, a really long time, and tons of effort to become very good at something.

Most people do not want to give their talent the time and effort required to develop it, especially when they have been in the workforce for years, and feel like it will take too long to really develop it. After all, here I am talking about ten years. Understand that Dr. Ericsson studies people who have attained world-class level in their domain: sports, music, art, science, etc., with most of them having started training at a young age (proof that it really pays to discover your talents as a child).

Ten thousand hours of practice in ten years is the equivalent of practicing four hours a day, five days a week for ten years. Now I know what you are thinking: "I have a job, maybe a family, a social life and other things that I have to attend to. I cannot afford to give four hours a day, five days a week to this." Do not worry about the time you are unable to give; focus on what you can commit to. A little effort put in on a consistent basis is better than a large effort put in occasionally, sort of like compound interest. Can you work on nurturing your talent thirty minutes to an hour a day? Once you know how much time you can give to it, then you are ready to create a plan.

> **Don't worry about the time you are unable to give; focus on the amount of time you can commit.**

Bill Rogers, CEO of SunTrust Bank in Atlanta, was once asked by a young leader in his organization how he still finds the time to develop himself in spite of his busy schedule. Bill responded, "I do not like it when people say they cannot find the time to develop themselves. You do not find or look for the time, you make the time." That is the bottom line; you have to organize your schedule to accommodate the development of your talent. By making the time, even if it's thirty minutes, five days a week to develop yourself, you can become a better analyst, communicator, salesperson, leader, accountant, software developer, project manager, technician, artist, and any other occupation you can think of.

The only way to get better is to work at getting better.
—*Kene Iloenyosi*

How to Nurture Your Talent

Gyms around the world make most of their money at the beginning of each year. If you have ever made a New Year's resolution to get fit, I am sure you can understand why. Most people with the holidays behind them, and a few extra and unwanted pounds on them, have the best of intentions to lose weight and get fit. This will be the year. They join their local gym, invest in workout clothes, make the time to work out, and start going to the gym. After their first few workouts, they get sore and decide to rest for a few days. The time they carve out is quickly filled up with something else. A few days turns into a week or so, and maybe they go back to the gym. They get sore again, and the cycle repeats itself. Most people quit in less than five weeks. Those who stick with it do so because they have two key things: a plan and some form of accountability, either a coach or a workout buddy. Those who hire a coach have a higher rate of success than all others. Success in nurturing your talents follows the same pattern. Let's talk about the three main steps to follow.

Three Key Steps to Effective Nurturing

1. Identify development areas.
2. Visualize and plan for success.
3. Practice effectively.

Step 1: Identify development areas

If you do not know what you want to nurture, you will expend your energy on useless efforts without making significant progress. Most people say that they want to be fit, but what exactly does that mean? Do they want to lose twenty pounds, be able to jog for thirty minutes three times a week, lose a certain amount of belly fat? When you are not specific, you will not be focused. You must ask yourself, "At what do I want to become an expert?" And to help you answer the question, you must discover your talent, figure out how you want to use this at work (subject of a later chapter), and identify the supporting skills.

You must ask yourself, "At what do I want to become an expert?"

1. Identify Your Talent

We dealt with this subject in the last chapter, and if you worked through the exercise you should have identified a few of your talents by now. Write out the talents you've discovered thus far.

_____

_____

_____

_____

_____

2. How Can/Will You Use This Talent at Work?

Talent does not operate in a vacuum; it needs to be used for a purpose. How can you use your talents in an organization? It may also be in a business. If you work for a company, then think of a role and a department in which your talent can be put to best use. List some below.

_____

_____

_____

_____

_____

3. Identify Supporting Skills

Talent is not enough! It is very important, but it is not enough. To be a high-level performer in your talent, you need to develop the key supporting skills. In Chapter 1, we discussed the difference between talent and skill. To identify the key supporting skills, you must identify how you want to use your talent (Step 2 above), and then zero in on the key elements needed for that role. For example, if you identified the ability to research things as a talent (very curious, and like to gather information on things of interest), supporting skills could be organizing information for others to use. This would entail learning to identify what others on your team need to know, simplifying and summarizing the content into easy to understand terms, etc. If you hate writing, you may want to look for a support person. You'd still have to organize content and learn to explain your content to them. List some supporting skills here.

———————————————————————————

———————————————————————————

———————————————————————————

———————————————————————————

4. Identify Your Resources

The resources you need may be people like a coach, accountability partner, a mentor, a class or course, someone doing what you want to do, books, podcasts, etc. List every resource you can think of, and then select the ones that will help you based on how you learn best. Some learn best when they read and do, others when they see and do, some when they hear and do, and others when they do. List your resources below.

———————————————————————————

———————————————————————————

———————————————————————————

———————————————————————————

Step 2: Visualize and Plan for Success

The list from Step 1 will help you develop a focused path of development. If you do not know where you want to go, any step will look good; but you will most likely end up going in circles. Now, it's time to plan.

1. Visualize: Identify What Success Will Look Like

This is critical; you must know what an expert in your field does. Find someone who has achieved what you want to achieve, and observe what they do and the effect or results of their action. You want to see the talent at work, and create an image of this in your mind. A number of people use vision boards to help them with this process, and it works. Others are able to develop and hold in their minds a clear and vivid picture of themselves as experts.

Visualization is a powerful personal development technique that has been used for centuries. When you hold an image in your mind long enough that it feels real to you, it motivates you to do all it takes to achieve that picture. Once you have that image, look at it and think about it often.

2. Plan Your Workout

This is very important. You have identified the talent and skills you want to develop, but how exactly will you develop them? How can you jog for thirty minutes if you have never done it before? Maybe you start by walking for thirty minutes three times a week for two weeks. This gets your heart rate up, your joints moving, and your muscles warmed up. Then you add some jogging into your walking; jog for one minute, and then walk for three or four minutes in the thirty-minute time allotted. You can do this for a week, and then increase your jogging time each week.

How do you become a better software programmer? Research programming languages out there and identify the ones you want to learn. Read a book on programming every month, or take an online programming course. If you will read a book, then you also want to write how long you will read every day or five days a week. Then, you plan to write in this new language five days a week for thirty minutes each time.

Or you want to become a better team leader or presenter? Your plan can look like this: read a book on this topic every month, read for thirty minutes five days a week. Select one thing from what you read and practice it every day for ten minutes, etc.

This is a plan you make on paper. I suggest you keep your plan simple so that it does not overwhelm you. Focus on developing one or two things at a time. If you work on too many things at the same time, you will not make significant progress in anything. Opt for going deep rather than broad.

Start Your Plan Here

_____
_____
_____
_____
_____
_____
_____
_____
_____
_____
_____
_____
_____

3. Plan Your Time: Make an Appointment with Yourself

The best plans are useless if you do not schedule them on your calendar. If you plan to read for thirty minutes five days a week, then go to your calendar and figure out when you will read each day, and put it on your calendar. Schedule time with yourself, and keep your appointment. If you take public transport to work, then you can commit that time to reading or listening to a podcast.

I speak and write for a living, and on my calendar I have my reading time, writing time, and the days when I speak in front of an audience for practice. I have done this for so long that I am able to move my daily schedule around.

Another reason why you should put your plan on your calendar is because life happens. You may have an incident such as illness or travel that throws you off schedule for a week or more. The daily notification on your calendar reminds you to get back on schedule as soon as possible. My reading notification pops up every day, whether I read or not. The daily notification is a reminder of how critical reading is to my success as a speaker and writer.

Write Your Schedule Here (Transfer to Calendar)

_____

_____

_____

_____

_____

_____

_____

_____

Step 3: Practice Effectively

You may have heard that practice makes perfect, and you agree with that. That statement is partially true. Practice makes permanent. So if you practice a skill in the wrong way, you make the wrong way permanent. Effective practice must be focused on practicing the correct thing, evaluating often, and then correcting practice action immediately. There has to be some sort of feedback mechanism that helps you ensure you are practicing correctly.

But, to practice correctly, you must start to practice. And the only way to start practicing well is to start small or in a fun way. In 2013, I made the dumb mistake of increasing the weight on my barbells because I saw a smaller person bench-pressing more than I was. I was working out with about 80 lbs. comfortably with just enough resistance during the repetitions to see the results on my body. I saw this smaller guy benching 140 lbs. What? If he can do that, surely I should be able to get to 120 lbs. Bad idea. I ended up hurting my rotator cuff, and could not bench-press for a very long time. This broke my routine and morale, and it has been hard to get back to lifting weights. So how do you avoid sabotaging your practice?

1. Play or Start Small (and Look for Fun Way to Start)

Depending on what you will practice, you want to start in a fun way if possible or start small. If your development requires reading, then make time to enjoy what you are learning. Do not read just to read; read to enjoy what you are reading. Read, think, ask questions, and as you continue in your day, keep thinking about what you read. If your practice involves taking a class or going back to school, find a way to enjoy the process. You can join a study group or online forum where others are discussing the topic you are learning. The sharing of ideas with like minds keeps the learning process fun and interesting as you share what you have learned, hear what others are learning, and go back to practice or think on what you heard from someone else. At work, it helps to find at least one person who wants to develop themselves. You can take turns sharing what you are learning over lunch twice a week.

Starting small gets you excited and warmed up to take on more. However, long-term growth requires more than this.

2. Push Past the Pain

My wife and I started running 5K races in 2014. Lucy trained with her friend Karla, who is an expert runner. During their practice runs, Lucy would sometimes complain of a little pain or running out of breath, and Karla would often respond with "push past the pain." Karla was not trying to be mean. As an expert runner she knew that Lucy was experiencing normal pains associated with running, and the only way to get past them and stop feeling them was to keep running. This made Lucy a stronger and faster runner. I adopted that mantra as well and would say it out loud to myself during my runs when I would feel out of breath and tempted to stop. I would keep running and soon enough, my strength would return.

In your development, the "pain" may be the time it takes to improve your talent, or looking at how much more work you'll have to do. It could be the fear of testing your new skills at work, or maybe just feeling bored with practice. At some point, you will be very tempted to throw in the towel. Most people quit at this point. Do not. Push past the pain. Push past the challenge or obstacle. When you hit the point where your practice starts to feel like really hard work, you have hit the phase where deep transformation happens. Again, do not quit. Push past the pain.

If you have ever seen the shows with people trying to lose weight, you will notice that they all lose some weight rapidly in the first few weeks of the program. They then get to a point where they stop losing weight as fast as they did initially. The same workout that helped them shed three pounds a week for the first three or four weeks is no longer effective in the program. They need to push harder. And in pushing harder, they may still end up losing weight at a slower rate. A lot of individuals get frustrated at this point and many give up. The ones who succeed are the ones who push past the frustration and stick to the process of increasing workout intensity.

Go on; "push past the pain."

3. Review and Adjust

I started my speaking career in 1997 as a youth pastor in Nigeria. I did this for a year and then went to Zambia as a missionary and pastor. I lived there for three years, and I was speaking on average about three times a week. Speaking is a talent for me, and I was comfortable speaking in front of people. I moved to America in 2001 and joined Toastmasters in 2004. I had never taken any class, workshop, or training in the art of speaking up until this time, and I had been speaking for about seven years. There were things I had to unlearn and relearn. I had to review, adjust, and relearn. One thing I soon realized was that I needed to speak with more vocal energy and vocal variety. No one ever told me that I often spoke in a monotone voice. I soon found out that there were many things I did not know. I was very comfortable speaking in front of an audience, but I was not very competent. The more I learned, the more I realized how incompetent I was. I now make the time every week to work on developing my communication talent and supporting skills.

If you are an analyst, then test your theories or assumptions. Create case studies or practice scenarios; see how fast you come up with results or solutions. Scientists are constantly evaluating what worked and what did not work in their experiments, and they keep adjusting different things in little increments to see the effect on their results. If it works they keep at it.

If it fails, they adjust.

If you are working on people skills and practicing how to listen effectively, maintaining eye contact and nodding are very important. You may unconsciously furrow your eyebrows when listening intently or when speaking passionately about something important. Others watching you may think you are upset because of your furrowed eyebrows. So although you are better at making eye contact and nodding, you now must learn to adjust your facial expressions to communicate interest. You can do this by making the effort to smile as you speak to or listen to people. This will take practice, and over time it will become part of you.

A communication coach I know was told he had to learn how to smile while working with his clients. He was not an angry or gruff person; he just had a default stern look when he was not smiling. It must have been awkward, but his practice routine was to smile at himself in the mirror many times a day. Today, he not only smiles when he speaks or works with his clients, but one seldom sees the stern look on his face.

4. Stretch Past Your Comfort

Growth happens outside our comfort zone.
—John Maxwell

If you ask people who have personal growth as a key part of their lives, they will tell you that when they stop growing, they feel like they are in a rut. A rut develops when we stay too long in our comfort zone. Growth happens when we are constantly reaching a few steps beyond where we are or what we know. There is a slight tension in this zone, and you do yourself a huge service by learning to be okay with this tension. Do not get too comfortable with your new level; keep looking for ways to grow, even in the smallest increment. Coach John Wooden said it best: "It is what you learn after you know it all that counts."

The way to ensure that you are constantly stretching is to keep setting new goals before you achieve the current goal you are working on. The best salespeople are always working on new leads while they turn cold leads into warm leads, warm leads into clients, current clients into repeat clients, repeat clients into raving fans, and raving fans into active referral sources. Every new client stretches them outside their comfort zone.

In your talent zone, you can always look for new skills that support your talent, or ways to increase your efficiency in working in your talent.

How Will You Stretch? Think Ahead

_____
_____
_____
_____
_____
_____
_____
_____
_____
_____
_____
_____
_____
_____
_____
_____
_____
_____
_____

Your talent needs to be nurtured, and that is work that you alone must do. Others may come alongside to support, coach, and encourage you, but you must lead the charge. It is your gift, your responsibility, and your life. If you do this, then you will be ready to put your talent to work in the service of humanity.

Journal

_____

_____

_____

_____

_____

_____

_____

_____

_____

_____

_____

_____

_____

_____

_____

_____

_____

_____

_____

_____

_____

_____

_____

_____

_____

_____

_____

_____

_____

CHAPTER SIX

Talent-Nurturing Environments

Our external shapes our internal,
which in turn shapes our external.
—Kene Iloenyosi

In the study of talent, there has been a long-standing debate on whether nature influences talent more than nurture or vice versa (nature vs. nurture). Proponents of nature believe that talent has more to do with a person's genetic makeup. They argue that since we do not get to choose our genes, it must follow that we also do not get to choose our talents. The nurture proponents on the other hand believe that talent is a result of the environment in which you grow up; your family influences as a child, your peer or social influences in your teen and young adult years.

I think the "nature vs. nurture" argument is absurd. It is not one or the other, but both working together; "nature + nurture" instead of "nature vs. nurture". Nature gives a person the talent, and the talent is nurtured to excellence. As has been made evident through this book and many written before it, no one was born an expert. Experts emerged after they had engaged in activities that developed their ability (talent) over a prolonged period of time.

In the earlier chapters, we looked in depth at the nature side of talent, and how to effectively nurture or develop your talents. This chapter will deal with the "nurture" environments that are optimal for talent development. They are:

1. The home environment
2. The school environment
3. The work environment
4. The friend environment

The Home Environment

This book was written primarily for young professionals—working, and living on their own. So why discuss their childhood? The environment in which a child grows up plays such a major role in how they view themselves and the world. It is critical to what an individual becomes. How this environment is structured can accelerate, delay, or prevent the development and maximization of talent in a child, and adversely affect how they function as adults. A participant at one of my Talent Discovery workshops had a hard time accepting the results of our talent discovery process that showed she had an artistic talent. As we delved deeper into why this was hard for her to accept, she admitted that as a child, her dad always made her feel like her art was never good enough. Not once did he tell her that her drawings were nice or affirm her artistic gift. His comments were often, "That was a good attempt, but it is not something at which you will excel." Her father was not abusive; he was very loving, but in this one area, he failed to see how his words affected his little girl. Here we were, almost thirty years later, talking about how this lady's childhood was still alive, negatively, in her present day. I would like to tell you that we nipped that voice at my session, but we did not. However, she did start the process of believing in her talent, and countering her dad's voice from her past.

Overcoming the "Nay" Voices

Step1: Identify the Root Voice

I am not a psychologist or therapist, but I have learned that the first step in overcoming any problem is to admit there is one. It is hard to build on a false premise; it will sabotage your efforts at some point. Do you feel a need to prove a point all the time? Are you always trying to please people to a fault? Do you internally struggle with the "I am not good enough" thought? Are you driven to succeed because of poverty in your childhood? There are so many things that could be listed here, but the main point is stepping back to ask yourself some hard questions that will help you understand why you act or think a certain way.

Step 2: Get a Reality Check

You must see yourself and your talent in a positive light. This is not always easy, but it is achievable. It starts with accepting that you have a talent or talents, and that you can do a lot of good with it. It is as simple as saying to yourself, "I really like working with numbers; it is a talent I was born with." You may have to write this down and read it to yourself many times a day. This starts to counter the wrong voice and gives power to the right voice, and in the process you build a new inner reality.

Step 3: Do What You Should

John Wayne said that "courage is being scared to death, but saddling up anyway." The fear voice will be louder at first, and you'll be tempted to turn down opportunities to use or develop your talent. Do not. Saddle up and work on it. Repeat your new positive statement and do what you should. You will not be great initially but over time (nurture), you will see your performance improving in the area of your talent.

Note: For some people, it may be necessary to see a therapist. Do what you need to do in order to be the best you can.

Some characteristics of homes with healthy, nurturing environments:
- Unconditional love from parents.
- Parents model appropriate disciplines.
- Parents affirm and support the development of the talent.
- Parents encourage and praise improvements in performance.
- Parents reward growth and results.

As you read the list above, it is obvious that key players involved in creating a talent-nurturing environment for a child are the parents—biological, adopted, foster, etc. The parent figure plays an important role.

The School Environment

A teacher affects eternity; they can never tell
where their influence stops.
—Henry Brook Adams

According to a University of Michigan study, children today spend about 7.5 hours every weekday at school, or 37.5 hours a week.[1] If the child sleeps 8 hours a day, it leaves them with 8.5 hours every weekday to be split between the drive to and from school, bathing and grooming, eating, doing homework, watching television, chatting with friends, playing on the computer, and of course interacting with parents and siblings. Children spend a considerable amount of time at school, as they rightly should, and are inevitably shaped in many ways by their experiences at school.

The school environment, second to the home environment, is a critical nurturing environment. It is important that we proactively create an environment that nurtures the best behavior in our students. It is equally important that we also create an environment that nurtures the talents in our students. And the earlier we get started, the better. Parents and teachers need to work together to nurture talent in their kids; one group cannot do it alone.

Teachers, after parents, are the most influential people in a child's life. True teaching has very little to do with transferring information. Technology is quickly changing how students learn. In developed nations, children with access to the internet can learn so much more on their own, and move ahead of the school's curriculum if they choose. In some schools today, students are given courses to read up or listen to online at home. Class time is then used primarily for discussion of what students read on their own, and resolving as a group any problems they encountered.

True and effective teaching therefore must spark an interest for learning in the child. Teach the child how to learn, help the child discover their strengths, and work with the child and parent to nurture that strength. Can you imagine what would happen if kids discovered their talents by the time they reached the fifth grade? Middle school and high school would then be focused on developing their talents through active participation in the subjects and activities that are needed by the talent, and developing the skills that work best with the talent. By the end of high school, most students would have a clearer picture on what career to pursue and would be able to decide if college, trade school, technical school, or an apprenticeship is the best next step to take. Our colleges today are filled with students in majors that they will not use when they graduate, racking up debt that will take them a long time to pay off, and who may go back to earn another undergraduate or postgraduate degree with more debt, thinking it will improve their chances of getting a better job.

We were not put on this earth to "get a job," but to fulfill a purpose. Our lives are bigger than just getting a job. Our lives are crying out for purpose, but most people have stifled this yearning by joining the hordes of people marching to a humdrum beat of simply surviving.

Teachers can have a significant impact on the lives of their students, if they choose to. Creating a talent-nurturing environment in their classrooms can help them achieve this goal. However, developing such an environment requires that the teacher believe in the premise of the Talent Revolution: that every child is born with a set of unique abilities, and our job as adults is to help them discover and develop those abilities. I know

I am asking a lot of teachers who already have so much on their plate, but we have to start dreaming about this first before we can make it a reality. I am sure some of the classroom practices of today would have sounded unrealistic to teachers in the 1970s and earlier. Did I mention that one of my talents is visualizing the future? So bear with me as I dream a little.

A TALENT-CENTRIC CLASSROOM (KENE'S DREAM)

In this classroom, teachers keep a Talent Journal on every student in their class, and this journal is passed on to other teachers as the child moves to the next grade. With cheaper accessibility to cloud technology, schools may opt to create an online Talent Journal where parents and teachers can go in and make notes, update notes, collaborate on nurturing activities, discuss handoffs from one teacher to another as the child moves through grade levels, and ultimately give the child access to this information at a certain agreed-upon age, like twelve or thirteen. Schools currently keep records on student performance and behavior, so adding this talent component is not that farfetched; it should be given a high priority.

Things teachers can do to create talent-nurturing environments:
- Partner and engage with parents. It is a team effort.
- Commit to learning new ways of engaging students.
- Be committed to creating a talent-nurturing environment.
- Help with visualization.
- Reward appropriately. Build self-esteem by rewarding excellence.

The Work Environment

Do what you love and you will love what you do. Most people will agree with this thought, but when pushed to live it out, most people will tell you to "get real." Get real!! How much more real can you get than working with your talent to do something you love? Most of us spend more time at work than we do at anything else, and unfortunately, most work environments are not set up to nurture the talents of their employees.

As stated in the introduction, the results of the Gallup Organization's 2015 employee engagement survey revealed that of the close to 100 million working adults in America, 50.8 percent are "Not Engaged," 17.2 percent are "Actively Disengaged," and only 32 percent are "Engaged." A direct link was found between engagement and the opportunity to use your talent at work. To help you understand why this is critical, let's list some of the characteristics of the people in the different categories.

50.8 percent are Not Engaged
- View work as merely a means to earn a paycheck
- Are not troublesome or disruptive at work but don't add immense value either
- Look forward to weekends, vacations, PTO etc.
- Not excited about Mondays
- Always wish they were doing something else but can't say what

17.2 percent are Actively Disengaged
- View work as a hostile environment
- Are out to undermine the team or company
- Gossip a lot
- Contribute most to shrinkage
- Do enough to remain on the payroll

32 percent are Engaged
- Work for them is exciting and passionate
- They are the creative and innovative ones
- Focused on adding value to team and company
- Work harder and longer than others because they love what they do
- Are always looking for better ways of doing things
- They are the driving force of the company and the economy

Jim Clifton, chairman and CEO of Gallup, wrote in his book *The Coming Jobs War*, "If companies double their number of engaged employees, they'll double the number of ideas and commercial energy running through the national grid of interconnected workplaces." I agree with Mr. Clifton. To make this a reality, however, employers and employees must do their best to ensure that most team members use their talents in their roles at work.

Tammy had been a project manager for many years and recently took a sales position with a new employer. As we talked about her work life, it was obvious that she was a strong process-oriented thinker; she was always looking to organize and improve systems and processes. During the interview for her current job, the company president asked her to take a sales position instead of the project manager role for which she originally applied. The money was more than she made in her past job, but she was not a sales person, had never been one, and was not planning to become one. But the money was good. She took the job. "I want to get to the executive level, and I think learning to be a sales person will help," she said as we discussed why she took the job. I did not bother arguing whether her thinking was right or wrong, but one thing was clear to both of us: the company president was not getting the best of this employee.

This lady is not enjoying her sales position but has found a way to make it work. She spends time improving processes she interacts with in her role; she approaches sales calls in a problem-solving manner (which means she will sometimes make recommendations that will not lead to a sale).

This company president has unknowingly created a not-engaged employee who will work to meet her sales goals without being fully utilized at work. Increasing the number of engaged employees should be the goal of every employer.

Engaged employees work in their strength, and as such they:
- Enjoy their work
- Are more productive (get more done in less time)
- Learn faster
- Are the source of innovation
- Are actually healthier and happier than others

Creating a Talent-Centric Work Environment

Step 1: Hire for Talent over Skill

The resume is and should be what gets an employer interested in a prospective employee. The problem with this is that resumes are a chronicle of a person's past work experience and achievements. If most people are not engaged at work, and are constantly looking for a better position, all they are doing is using experiences they did not love to try and find a job they will love. I call this the resume trap. A friend of mine complained to me about recruiters calling her for positions she did not want even though the money was always good. When we looked into this, her resume was filled with work experience from past positions she did not love.

How then do we change this? The first thing we must understand, and accept, is that employers are not primarily responsible for helping employees discover their talent; that is the employee's responsibility. That said, the employer should encourage employees to discover their talents and find ways to use them at work. They should be open to moving employees out of roles that do not align with their strength, and into roles that do.

During the hiring process, employers should educate themselves on what types of talents/strengths would be critical for the open position, and then design questions that will identify these qualities during the interview. They may ask prospective employees to take strengths-assessment tests ahead of an in-person interview. The presence of relevant strengths combined with related work experience should bring employers closer to an ideal hire.

I am not saying that skills do not matter, they do. My view is that your skills should support your talent. When employees work and lead with their talents, the organization gets a higher return on investment. When people work only in a skill area, they will not be fulfilled, and if they work hard at it, they will at some point experience burnout.

Make hiring for talent a priority.

Step 2: Position Properly

I liked jigsaw puzzles as a child and enjoyed solving them with friends. When working on the more difficult puzzles, there would be times when a puzzle piece looked like it fit in a particular space. It was an almost fit. And as a kid, because it almost fit, I would try to force the piece in. The result was never as smooth as the other perfect fits.

Hiring the person with the right talent is the first step. The next step is making sure there is a good fit between the person and the role. I define a good fit as a position in which the employee spends 70–80 percent of their time working on tasks that require the use of their talents. I say 70–80 percent because most jobs will always have necessary elements that we may not be thrilled to do but have to address. Try to minimize the mundane. If you use the 80/20 rule (Pareto principle), you'll find that only about 20–30 percent of your tasks account for the critical elements of your job. Spend most of your time doing what matters most, and then plan a good time to work through the tasks that are not critical to your success. Do not ignore these minor things, because if they are ignored long enough they will cause you more trouble. Give them time, just not the bulk of your time.

If there are tasks that can be eliminated completely without affecting the productivity of the employee, I say get rid of them.

Step 3: Eliminate Poor Managers

The effect of bad management on the overall morale of a team cannot be overstated. If an organization has a high rate of employee turnover, the fault is not with the employees, it is the employer. So who then is the employee and who is the employer? This may sound like a strange question, but it isn't. Everyone who works for an organization is an employee (even the owners of a company). However, the higher an employee climbs in an organization, the more influence they exert on the organization. The employer therefore becomes an aggregate of all the people who exert influence in the organization. If you are a low-level employee, and you manage one person, you can be referred to as the employer. CEOs and presidents wield enormous influence on an organization, but they too can be fired.

Talented people will not stay in a toxic work environment (unless they are the cause of the bad vibes). They know they can find another job because they are very good at what they do. Even your "actively disengaged" and "not engaged" employees will leave your company once they find a better alternative. If you are serious about developing a good work environment, then you cannot think twice about releasing employees with a lousy attitude, even the talented ones. Warn them once and then train them. If they do not change, fire them. I am unapologetic about this; get rid of your "stinka-thinkas."

Step 4: Let Them Play

In 2015, I got to do some executive communication coaching work at a tech company in Atlanta. I had heard about the so-called hip and youthful work environments and this was my first time to experience one. They had foosball tables, dart boards, beanbags, couches, scooters, a slide that connected two floors, and even beer in the fridge. I asked why the company allowed people to drink at work and a senior HR team member said, "We hire talented people, and if having a beer helps them unwind and be more productive, why not?" When he said that, it hit me; when you hire good people, you don't need to control them. Let them loose in their area of strength, and you will be amazed at how much they produce.

Daniel Pink, in his book *Drive*, teaches that the three key elements to personal motivation are "autonomy, mastery and purpose."[2] Talented people want freedom in how they work. If they give you the results you need, get out of their way.

Jim Clifton's comment is worth repeating; ***"If companies double their number of engaged employees, they'll double the number of ideas and commercial energy running through the national grid of interconnected workplaces."***

Do not underestimate the power of an engaged employee. If you want raving customers, focus on developing engaged employees.

The Friend Environment

Jim Rohn said that "you are the average of the five people with whom you spend the most time." Maybe this is the reason why some people don't want any friends. The people with whom we spend the most time will determine the outcome of our lives because they will either encourage us to stretch, grow, and become better, or they will discourage our efforts to stretch, grow, and become better. Trust me, you want friends that will encourage and not discourage you. You want friends that you can trust, and who will not be envious of your drive to develop. You want friends who are as driven as you are, in the same or in a different domain.

Our friends, to a large extent, determine our outlook on life. If we have negative and small-minded friends, sooner or later we will start to think like them. I once heard a story of a man who grew up in a small, rural town. His childhood friends were satisfied growing up and living in the same town, but this man had a belief that he could outgrow the town. As teenagers, his friends ridiculed him for wanting to become a "city person." He had a choice to make; he could leave the town and take his chances in the big city. Or he could cave in and let go of his city dreams. Well, he chose to leave his friends and leave the town. Life in the city was not easy, but it offered the challenges he desired.

He went back to visit his little town after five years in the city. He met up with his old friends and they all wanted to hear about the city. In a very short time it dawned on him that although he loved his childhood friends, they could not be a part of his future. They now had very little in common. In five years, he had learned so much about the world, met people from other cultures and countries, and was a very different person from the guy who left five years earlier. His childhood friends noticed the change as well. His outlook on life was so different from theirs, and so were his interests and goals.

Parents must teach their children to choose friends wisely. This is a skill that must be learned independent of talent development. As children, it is easy to get caught up in peer pressure and the need to fit in.

Parents can make a difference in the lives of their children by developing a strong relationship that grows and transforms as the child grows. Listening to your children without always correcting or giving advice is a sure way to build a solid relationship. I am not an advocate of parents who want to be friends with their children at all costs. That is destructive to the child. Children need parents to be parents and not their friends. Parents can be friendly with their kids, but must set healthy boundaries for them. The boundaries and discipline actually help the children understand and develop a healthy self-esteem and equips them to set their own boundaries.

My nephew was very careful about who made it into his inner circle. Like most kids and teenagers, he liked his video games and loved football. His parents did their best to buy him the games he wanted. He would often have different friends over to play video games. In the process of play, he found ways to ask about their favorite subjects and their grades. He was able to quickly determine those who valued play over studies and those who valued studies over play. He drastically reduced the time he spent with those who valued play more than studies. He was never unkind to them, but they would not be close friends. He was focused on playing football and going to college to study electrical engineering. He eventually quit football in his freshman year to focus on his studies.

Protect your talent by building friendships that nurture it.

Chapter Exercise: Evaluate Your Environment

Work on these exercises in a notepad or private journal.

Home Environment

1. Did you grow up in an affirming and encouraging home?
    Yes __ \ No __
    Think about the home environment in which you grew up, get a notepad, and write out what type of environment it was.
2. How has this environment affected the type of adult you have become? Are you confident or lacking in confidence? Are you a risk taker or risk averse? Are you insecure or very secure in who you are? Are you optimistic or pessimistic? Think through your positive or negative attitudes and try to identify where you learned them.
3. How will you change the negative things you have identified?
    You may need to read books or see a counselor or coach. Make a list of what you need to do, and start doing them.
4. If you are a parent, what type of home environment are you creating for your kids?

School Environment

If you are a teacher, what are you doing to encourage and nurture the development of talent in your students? You can:
1. Read and learn more about talent in your spare time. This will help you with the discovery process.
2. Keep a journal in which you make notes about the peculiar traits that you notice in your students.
3. Have a meeting with the parents of your students, and talk with them about discovering the talents in their children.

4. Tell the parents what you have observed in their children, and see if the child displays the same traits (or others) at home.
5. Identify extracurricular activities that will help the child nurture their talents.

Work Environment

1. Do you use your talents at work?
2. If yes, what percentage of your work requires the use of your talents?
3. If no, what will you do about it?
4. Do you feel appreciated by your managers?
5. Do you verbally appreciate the people you work with?
   Write some things you will do to appreciate the people with whom you work. It may be thanking them for helping you with something, recognizing a particular contribution they have made to a project or the team, or just letting them know you are glad they are part of the team.

Friend Environment

1. Make a list of your closest friends. Don't worry if you have more than five.
2. Under each friend, list the things that are most important to them in life. What do they want to achieve?
3. Make a short list of what you want to achieve.
4. Do you and your closest friends have similar priorities? The list may not be in the same field and order, but they do need to be close.
5. Do your close friends know what you want to achieve?
6. Are your friends helping or hampering your personal and professional growth?
7. Are you helping or hampering the personal and professional growth of your friends?
8. Do you need to make new friends or dive deeper into the relationships you have?

Journal

_____

_____

_____

_____

_____

_____

_____

_____

_____

_____

_____

_____

_____

_____

_____

_____

_____

_____

_____

_____

_____

_____

_____

_____

_____

_____

_____

_____

_____

CHAPTER SEVEN

Apply Your Talent

The individual who knows his own aptitudes,
and their relative strengths, chooses more intelligently
among the world's host of opportunities.
—*Johnson O'Connor*

t was almost 2 p.m. and we had spent most of the morning session helping attendees identify at least one talent from their childhood. Alex had identified that he enjoyed building things with his hands as a child, and still enjoys this as an adult. He also loves to see old or damaged things restored. He currently worked as a manager at an auto body shop and was not very excited about his job. As we discussed what he really longed to do for work, his answers revolved around working with his hands. His current job removed him completely from hands-on activity, and he was not happy about it. "I want to get back to working on the cars." It was an obvious choice; the downside was that it technically would be a demotion, with a lower position and less money.

Alex eventually decided to follow his talent, and got a job with a different company as a collision repair technician. Although this was a lower position, Alex was making about the same amount of money as he did in his previous job, but he was finally doing what he was good at and more importantly, what he loved. He found a way to put his talent to work.

Put Your Talent to Work

We were created to fulfill a purpose, not just work a job.
—Kene Iloenyosi

The ultimate aim of discovering and nurturing talent is for you to engage it in a meaningful career. Your talent mix is an indicator of the type of work you should pursue. There are people who believe that with training, we can be great at anything. They are partially correct. But why not invest in what I already have? I am a proponent of using our talents in the work we do. I believe that you give your best when your talent is engaged in work you enjoy.

So, how do you find the right job or career after you have discovered and developed your strongest talents? There are four options:

1. Change roles within the same company/organization.
2. Move to another company/organization.
3. Start your own company.
4. Volunteer with a nonprofit.

Change is not always easy or pleasant, but it is necessary to get you into a fulfilling career. It may not be easy but it is still doable. Surround yourself with people who will encourage you in your move, and forge on.

Let's explore each option.

1. Change Roles within the Same Company

Remember Tammy from the previous chapter? She was the project manager who took a sales position because of the money. Talking about the benefits of using one's talent at work inspired her to ask me, "So how do I move into my desired project management role?"

Tammy had interviewed for a project manager role and had been offered a sales role because the president needed a sales position filled. I told her that if the project manager role was open, she should talk with her boss about moving to it. She rolled her eyes and said, "My boss does not seem concerned about filling that position." I asked her if he was concerned with saving money. "Of course he is."

"Well," I said, "you have talked about all the processes you have made efficient that have saved the company a lot of wasted time. Is there a monetary value to that?"

"Yes," she said.

"Good. Document every process you have improved and what it has saved the company. Then plan a meeting with your boss to discuss this. The focus of your discussion should be where you can best add the most value to the company, not where you want to go."

It is sometimes easier to change positions within the same company, especially if it is a large one. There is a misconception that young professionals today are not interested in a thirty-five-year career with the same company. There is some truth to that, but the real issue is boredom. When they get bored with their jobs, they won't stick it out like our parents did. They change companies because they think their present company will frown at their desire to move. A number of Fortune 500 companies have mitigated the turnover by being proactive about moving their younger employees around the company, sometimes around the world. I find it hard to imagine that a sensible human resource executive would frown at an opportunity to utilize an employee's strength in a way that immensely benefits the organization.

If there is a position at your current company that appeals to you, for which you are a good fit, and one that enables you to bring great value to the organization, then consider moving to that position if at all possible.

I suggest you follow this approach:

1. If possible, volunteer to work on some projects from the department or team to which you desire to move. This will be proof that you can do the work well.

2. If that is not possible, you will need some other type of proof. Can you volunteer your talent in the service of a nonprofit? This will help prove you can do the job.

3. If options 1 and 2 are not possible, you will have to make a strong case for how you can add value to the organization by moving to this position.

4. List the benefits to the company, of your being in this desired position. The conversation must first be about the value to the organization, not you. If you have a monetary value to each benefit in terms of savings or revenue, add that.

5. Have a clear understanding of the company's vision and current goals, and base the conversation on using your talents to help the company meet its goals or achieve its vision.

6. Have a very clear understanding of the role you are asking for, the tasks that require your talent, and those that do not. This way you will not be blindsided by questions about the role; you do not want to go into the discussion unprepared.

7. Plan your presentation, keep your discussion short and focused on points relevant to the company and even the person with whom you will be speaking. Practice adequately for this meeting, and prepare for questions.

This is a suggested approach, and there are no guarantees that an employer will approve your proposal. Some would argue that you might be fired because the HR folks now know you are not happy in your current position. That is a possibility. But it is a risk worth taking if there is a role at which you would excel while bringing immense benefits to your employer.

If you are not comfortable taking this approach, and are not excited about your current role, then consider the next option.

2. Move to Another Company/Organization

If you are not happy in your current role and cannot move to a better-fitting role within your current organization, you might seriously consider looking for the right position at a different organization.

Moving to a new company means looking for a new job, and a lot of people are afraid of taking this step. They are hindered by the prevalent notion that there are few jobs out there and companies are not hiring. There is always news of one company or another laying off employees. While this is a fact, we must never forget the primary reason why corporations exist: **to make a profit for its owners by providing a service or product.** Jobs are created in order to fulfill this primary reason in a profitable way. Anyone who can help a corporation increase its profits either by generating more revenue or decreasing expenses will always, and I repeat, always find a job. The nonprofit sector is not focused on profit, but the same principle applies.

If you understand this fundamental truth about corporations, and your talents help a corporation generate more profit, you will be hired. I have seen companies that were "not hiring," but still created a position in order to hire someone they believed would bring immense value to the organization. This happened to a friend of mine, Jason. He had shut down his small business that he was not enjoying; there was no fulfillment in what he did and he could not continue with it. Jason had always been great with people and knew how to build and deepen relationships. In his other previous jobs, he did well in sales positions. The CEO of a tech company based out of Dallas heard about him from a mutual friend. His company was not hiring, but he knew a value-adding person when he saw one. Jason filled the bill. He reached out to Jason and offered him a job that was aligned with his talents. Jason took the job.

So, how do you find the ideal job for you? I may not be an official career coach, but here is some advice that has worked for many. The steps below assume you have discovered your talents and how best to use them in an organization.

Step 1: Rewrite Your Resume

In the introduction section of this book, I talked about the resume trap. If you pull out your resume and look at it, I can bet that you would not want to spend the rest of your life working in most or all of the past roles you listed. There are different schools of thought on how to write a resume, and I am not going to debate the best format in this book. My opinion is that a resume that reflects the use of your talents and highlights the value you have brought to past employers will be much better than most of the resumes out there today.

Rewrite your past roles in the context of how you were able to use your talents (if you used them, that is), and the value you added to your employer. If you have not been able to use your talents at work, then I suggest you look for opportunities to do so. Do not expect to get paid for this, and do not let your primary work suffer. Another option could be to use your talents in the service of a nonprofit as a volunteer or, if possible, and depending on the talent, do some after-hours pro bono consulting for six months to a year. You want something that shows the value of your talent.

In your resume, include what I call your value proposition statement. This statement defines how your talents align with your core roles (or position for which you are applying) and how it serves the mission or priorities of the organization.

EXAMPLE: SALES MANAGER/DIRECTOR

My talents for understanding people, teaching, and spotting emerging trends make me very effective in my role as a sales manager. I use these talents to coach my sales team in areas where they need help, and to spot opportunities ahead of our competitors.

Step 2: Decide What You Will Do for Work

Do not just say you are looking for a job. What will you do in that job? How would you like to use your talents in an organization? If you don't know what you want, you will not know when you find it, or come close. Do not be like the lady who interviewed for a project manager position and ended up being offered, and taking, a sales position. You must be clear on how your talents can serve the organization, and what roles will fill that need. My goal is for you to be able to spend at least 80 percent of your time using your talents at work. You decide what percentage is agreeable with you.

In this step, you should also decide what industries, if any, are most desirable to you. If you do not like the insurance industry, I would not suggest taking a job there because it meets your talent engagement criteria. You still want to enjoy the company you work for. This may not seem very important to you, and that is okay.

Step 3: Research the Companies You Are Interested in

Identify the companies or industries in which you would like to work, and do your homework on them. Get a general view of the industry, what is going well, what is not, what the emerging trends are, the biggest players in the industry, etc. With specific companies, know what their vision and mission statements are and what goals they may currently be pursuing. These may be found on their website or other websites on which the company has been reviewed. You can also look online for interviews done by the CEO and other high-ranking executives. Watch as many as you can. You will see a pattern of thought; this will give you a sense of their priorities for the next year or next few years.

Step 4: Plan Your Pitch, and Then Pitch

Write resumes tailored to each organization and sell your value based on how your talents will help the company achieve the goals and priorities set by the senior executive team. If there are terms you heard repeated by the CEO and other executives that you can work into your resume or the cover letter, add it. The goal is to get you noticed.

Plan your pitch to the human resource director (or whoever is hiring) with their priorities top of mind. Using the **WIIFT Rule** (What's In It For Them), start with what you have observed are their key priorities as a company. Then talk about your talents in the context of how you can help achieve those priorities. Be specific in what you hope to achieve in the role for which you are applying; do not just say you will help increase revenue or reduce expenses. Talk about how your actions in the role will impact the company, and increase profits or reduce expenses.

Keep your points to three to four key points that tie into what is most important to them. Prepare for questions that may be asked of you. Write out all questions you anticipate and then rehearse how you will answer them when asked.

When you are prepared, start calling to make an appointment with the hiring person. Make sure your LinkedIn profile is written in a talent-centric manner that highlights your value to prospective employers. If you aren't familiar with LinkedIn, please go to www.linkedin.com to find out.

3. Start Your Own Company

The self-employed world is one in which I have spent most of my adult life, starting with my first venture in Nigeria at the age of twenty-one. Research has shown that a higher percentage of millennials and Gen. Zs will choose the self-employed/entrepreneurial path than those in generations before them. That said, the details on how to start a business are not what this book is about, and so I will focus specifically on making the transition from paid employment to talent-centric self-employment.

Most of the ventures I started were driven by the need to make money for myself as a bachelor, and then for my family after I got married. None of them had anything to do with my talents, at least not directly. I am good at connecting with people, communication, and futuristic thinking; and I did get to use my talents sometimes. But the businesses were not based on my strongest talent, which is communication. Since 2004, I have dreamt of being a professional speaker, but just never had the courage to make the step. In 2007 while running our creative service business, I made the firm commitment to get into professional speaking as a business. I made the commitment, and went full time into it in 2012. It took me five years because I had to figure out what topic I was passionate about, learn about the topic, write a book on it, and then officially start the business. This was my journey; the transition time may be much shorter for you, depending on what you want to do.

It is very important to remember that I am talking about starting a business that depends on your talent. If you are gifted in art, start a graphic design company. If you like to cook, become a chef or open a restaurant. If you are good at process/analytical thinking and you know a specific industry well, become a consultant to fix broken processes. Michael Gerber, author of *The E-Myth*, said that it is sometimes better for a person to start a business that does not depend on their talent because they will most likely spend all their time working in the business instead of on the business, with the end result being burnout and business failure because the provider, in trying to produce what is required for the client, oftentimes ends up neglecting the other parts of the business that ensure its long-term success. This happens because those aspects of the business are not things the person enjoys doing, and they may not yet have the resources to hire an extra person. I have seen this happen many times. I have also seen people who figured out a way to make it work. They planned their schedule efficiently and set out time to do the needed tasks like returning client calls, reconciling bank accounts, marketing their services or products, and running errands. They did not enjoy these aspects but planned for them. A lot has also changed since the book *The E-Myth* was written; it is much easier and cheaper to hire virtual assistants who can do most things you need done at a fraction of the cost of hiring a full-time employee. Another alternative I have seen is partnering with another person. So, it is very possible to start and run a business that depends directly on your talent.

So, how do you make the transition from paid employment to self-employment?

Step 1: Decide and Commit

As obvious as this seems, I still must say it. You cannot start a business if you do not know what you want to do. It is important to look at as many options as possible, but don't get caught up in "analysis paralysis." You have to make a decision and commit to it.

With your talent inventory at hand, think through how you would want to use it/them in a business. Look around and see if you can meet with, talk to, or read up on someone doing what you want to do. Some people may see you as their competition and not want to talk with you. Do not let that get to you; find those who are willing to help. You will have more luck with someone who is much further along in the business than someone who is just starting out but is ahead of you by a year or so.

Do your research; decide exactly how you will use your talent in your business, who you will serve and how. Be as clear as you possibly can.

Step 2: Start Your Business Part Time

If you have developed your talent to a market valuable level, then I would recommend starting it part time. You can work nights and weekends and use some of your vacation time when necessary. A friend of mine is a sales executive in her daytime work and a designer and tailor part time. She makes wedding and prom gowns and, yes, she sometimes has little time for a social life. She knows what she wants to achieve, and is making the sacrifice necessary. You cannot always have everything at the same time, so choose what is most important.

There are some businesses that are next to impossible to conduct in the evenings and weekends, especially if your clients will be other businesses. If this is the case, then cut back on your expenses, make sure you have enough savings to last at least a year, and then launch out into the deep. Wake up every single day and pursue clients with all you have.

Step 3: Go Full Time

You know you are ready to go full time when your part-time efforts will no longer sustain the business. This happens after you have acquired some clients, they like your service, and they start to tell others about you. This is a good problem; unfortunately, it can also be a reason why many businesses fail. There is just so much that one person can handle, and many fail to recognize that limit. For example, when you are part time, your limit may be five clients at the same time. When those clients like your work and each of them brings you a new client, you all of a sudden go from five to ten clients. You are no longer able to deliver work on schedule. You stay up much later at night to get the work done. Your productivity at both jobs starts to slip. Your clients that used to praise you start wondering if you are getting lazy and before you know it, they all leave you.

When you are approaching your limit, it is time to quit your day job. Don't take a vacation. I have seen people who decided to take two weeks off before going full steam into their business. This is a mistake; if you have momentum on your side, why stop? When you take a vacation, you spend some time in the planning phase and some time getting out of vacation mode. You may end up losing a month. When you go full time, go all the way. Start your day on time and get a lot more done. Free up some of your evenings and weekends in order to get sufficient rest.

MY WIFE LUCY'S STORY

My wife started her graphic design business while she had a full-time job, and worked nights and weekends to serve her clients. When we decided to shut down my moving company so that I could help grow the design business, it was similar to leaving a job; we were going to lose the income from that business. Since she still had a full-time job, we trimmed our combined expenses to what her salary could afford: got rid of the second car, took no vacations, cut back on eating out and doing anything that was unnecessary. It was tight for a while, but that was what had to be done. She left her full-time job when we were generating enough revenue in the design business to pay her what she earned at her day job. The immediate relief at this time was that she no longer had to work late nights and weekends; we still had to live on a lean budget for a few more years as we grew the business to the point where we could eventually hire another designer. I didn't take a salary for a few years, and we went for about a year without health insurance. Hey, you do what you have to do! We are in a much better place today, but it would not have been possible if we did not make the sacrifices up front.

4. Volunteer Your Talent

Some of you reading this book may not be just quite ready to change direction. That is okay. If you would still like an opportunity to put your talent to work, without leaving your current position or starting a business, you can volunteer your talent at work or with a nonprofit organization. We mentioned volunteering your talents at work in a previous section, so I will discuss using your talent for a nonprofit in this section.

Volunteer-based organizations do not always have the funds to pay people for their services, but require most of the roles needed in a for-profit organization. This presents an amazing talent development and engagement opportunity. I know people who use their organizational abilities, administrative abilities, relational abilities, and communication abilities, etc., to help volunteer organizations. It's a win-win; the volunteer gets to use their talent and make difference, and the organization reaps the benefit of what the individual does.

I often advise people in the workforce looking for opportunities to develop their talent, to find a nonprofit that has a need for that talent and volunteer to serve there a few hours a week. For your talent to be marketable, it cannot be average. Using it in a volunteer scenario gives you the opportunity to develop it.

TOASTMASTERS INTERNATIONAL

I am part of an organization called Toastmasters International. If you have never heard of it, it is an organization that helps people develop leadership and communication skills (go to www.toastmasters.org). The development happens in clubs scattered around the world. Each club has anywhere from eight members on the low end to as many as sixty members on the high end, and is led by a Club President and an executive committee of six other team members.

- Four to six clubs are grouped together to form an Area overseen by an Area Director.
- Four to six Areas are grouped together to form a Division overseen by a Division Director.
- Six to twelve Divisions are grouped together to form a District. In many cases, the geographical spread of a District can be as small as a number of sections of a city grouped together (New York City) to as large as countries grouped together (all countries in West Africa). A District is overseen by a senior district leadership team headed by a District Director.
- Districts are grouped together to form Regions, and each is represented (not led) by an International Director.
- The International Directors, along with four International Officers plus the CEO of the organization, constitute and serve on the Toastmasters Board of Directors, which is led by the International President.

If your head is spinning with this information, I totally understand; it took me a while to understand it too. Here is what I want you to see: all the positions I mentioned, from Club President to the International President (except CEO), are filled by volunteers. They have their regular jobs; most have a family and still put in plenty of time to serve within the organization.

I served as District Governor (now District Director) over the state of Georgia (USA), and it was like a second job with travel requirements. The higher up you go in the organization, the more travel is required of you. It is a lot of hard work, but it gives many of us opportunities to develop leadership and communication skills and many other organizational skills. These skills are talents for some members, and many of us have used serving in these offices as a platform to develop these talents. I sharpened my communication talent in my capacity as a District Officer by speaking at numerous large events over a period of seven years. The transition to professional speaking was made much easier because of this experience. I have other friends who have become communication skills coaches and volunteer leadership Coaches.

Do not underestimate the value and power of volunteering your talents to a worthy cause. As you give it away, you will get so much more in return in the form of experience, satisfaction of being part of serving a cause you care about, recognition, etc. The more you give, the more you get. It is a principle of life.

Stop Working for a Paycheck

We spend the bulk of our time at work; it is therefore critical that we spend that time engaged in something we are good at and love. Stop working for a paycheck, you were created for more than that.

For every profession imaginable, there are people with the base talent for it. Leave money out of the equation; just think about the profession, no matter how menial or how specialized. The person in a menial job with a talent for that job will be happier than a person in the same job without the talent. The person in a menial job who has a talent for that job can develop their talent to a level where they can move to a better job that requires the same talent, or add skills that can help them build a business out of that menial job. I read a quote that was attributed to former Associate Justice of the US Supreme Court Justice William J. Brennan Jr., and he said that "there are no menial jobs, only menial attitudes." A person's attitude toward their talent and work will determine what they end up doing with it.

"There are no menial jobs, only menial attitudes."

Ever heard of the company College Hunks Hauling Junk? Removing junk from people's homes and offices may be considered a menial, low-paying job, but founders Omar Soliman and Nick Friedman have turned this into a multimillion-dollar company. I know a former day laborer who now runs his own landscaping business, and former housekeepers who now run their own housecleaning business. And they all love what they do and have found a way to expand it and create employment for others.

If you are not fulfilled in your current job, then use what you have learned in this book to find and do work that you love. I encourage you to ask yourself the hard questions: "Do you love your job and can you be great at it?" If the answer is no, make the commitment to change your situation. You have a set of unique talents that, if developed and used at work, will bring you immense joy and fulfillment.

Chapter Exercise

Are you thrilled at the thought of remaining in your current career for the rest of your life?

_____

_____

_____

_____

If you answered no above, will you commit to putting your talent to work?

_____

_____

_____

_____

What will you need to do to make this happen?

_____

_____

_____

_____

_____

_____

_____

Who will you ask to hold you accountable?

_____

_____

The Talent Revolution

After Sipola finished her MBA, she was offered a job at a major bank as a process design consultant. Who knew that such an aptly titled position existed? A recruiter had looked at her profile on LinkedIn, noticed the type of work she was doing with small businesses and nonprofit organizations, and reached out to her about this position. Her days are spent figuring out how various bank processes can be improved. Most days at work, she feels like a kid in a candy store. That is the power of putting your talent to work. At the time I was writing this chapter, she had started a new job at a different company doing the same thing but at a more senior position. In talking about her career future, she said, "Now I understand what you mean by finding work that you can do for the rest of your life; I've found my life career."

She will most likely change jobs over the course of her career, but she has found "what" she will do for the rest of her life. And all this started because she first identified her talent. This is where it starts; it is not rocket science. Anyone at any age can discover their talent and put it to work in a fulfilling career.

An Update on
Finding Your Sweet Spot

Since *Finding Your Sweet Spot* was published in 2012, many people have made amazing discoveries and changes in their lives based on something they read in the book. I know a lady who is a highly paid consultant, who after reading my book started exploring her childhood and reconnected with her gift for sewing. She still works as a consultant but uses her talent to make unique craftwork for people.

In the fall of 2012, at a local fair in my city, a couple walked up to me. The wife, with a look of sheer delight, said, "I had been thinking about getting out of the restaurant business. After reading your book, I knew I was not in my sweet spot and had to get out. We've put it on sale and are already discussing with a potential buyer." They sold it before the end of 2012. This lady was in her sixties and was taking the step to discover her talent and where best to put it to use.

In 2014, I ran into her husband at a Starbucks shop and asked after her. He said, "Nancy has always been a numbers person and enjoys analyzing stocks. She took a class on trading stocks and now spends her time managing a portfolio of stocks for our family. She loves what she does."

It does not matter if you are twenty or sixty; we all want to do work we love and which we can be very good at. That is why I am starting a Talent Revolution.

The Talent Revolution

In 2013, I added a free downloadable Talent Discovery Worksheet to my website. I put it there as a quick-start resource for anyone interested in discovering their talent. I was surprised at the countries from which people were downloading this document: Germany, England, Kenya, South Africa, Nigeria, China, Holland, Denmark, Canada, and many cities within the United States. The frequency with which this document was downloaded indicated that many people around the world had a desire to discover their talents. I knew I was onto something, and there was more that I could do to help people.

The Talent Revolution is a movement of young adults interested in discovering their talents, developing them and using them in a fulfilling career.

I am tired of hearing people complain about not liking their jobs and wishing they could find what they can really enjoy. Millennials and Generation Zs are now the dominant generations in the workplace, and stand the best chance of doing work they love for a much longer time.

If young adults around the world catch onto this, and apply their talents to their careers, I believe we can increase the productivity of many companies and, in turn, nations. The most innovative people are those who get to work in their talent zone; can you imagine what would happen if more young adults unleashed their innate talents at work?

Technology is rapidly changing how people work, and the types of work people do. And many people believe that this shift will lead to the loss of many jobs, with machines and computers becoming more efficient at performing many tasks. This is true and is an inevitable consequence of mankind's progress. It is pointless to try and fight it, and much better to embrace the change and figure out how to use your talents to take advantage of it. No matter the level of technological advancement we experience, there will always be a need for humans and our talents. The big question we need to ask ourselves is, "How will I use my talent in my generation?" Young adults must stay up to date on emerging trends, and must constantly look for ways to stay relevant. The way we use our talents may change but the one thing that will not change is the presence of talent in humans and the need to express it.

Join the movement.

Discover your talent and put it to work.

JOIN THE TALENT REVOLUTION

www.talentrevolution.me

Notes

Introduction

1. www.gallup.com/corporate/177680/gallup.aspx
2. Johnson O'Connor created a nonprofit scientific research and educational organization over ninety years ago. He wanted to help individuals discover their natural potential, and be able to use it for greater personal benefit. With their aptitude testing service, the organization has helped hundreds of thousands of individuals still in school, seeking employment, or making midlife career changes to find direction in educational and career planning.
3. Broadley, Margaret E. "Your Natural Gifts." Atlantic Monthly (June 1931): 00-00.

Chapter 1

1. Isaacson, Walter. *Einstein, His Life and Universe.* New York: Simon & Schuster, 2007, 31.

Chapter 3

1. Ruthsatz & Detterman (2003): 509.
2. Feldman & Katzir (1998).
3. Abbott et al. (2002).
4. Belfiore, Michael. "Orbit on a Shoestring," in *Rocketeers: How a Visionary Band of Business Leaders, Engineers, and Pilots Is Boldly Privatizing Space.* Harper Collins, 2007. 166–195.
5. Winner, Ellen. *Gifted Children: Myths and Realities.* Basic Books, 1996.
6. www.cbsnews.com/news/60-minutes-overtime-12-year-old-jazz-prodigy-joey-alexander/
7. Kearney, Kevin James, and Cassidy Yumiko Kearney. *Accidental Genius.* Woodshed Press, 1998.
    Winner, Ellen. *Gifted Children: Myths and Realities.* Basic Books, 1996.

Chapter 5

1. K. Anders Ericsson, ed. *The Road to Excellence: The Acquisition of Expert Performance in the Arts and Sciences, Sports, and Games.* New Jersey: Lawrence Erlbaum Associates, Inc., 1996.

Chapter 6

1. www.ur.umich.edu/0405/Dec06_04/20.shtml
2. Pink, Daniel. *Drive: The Surprising Truth About What Motivates Us.* Riverhead Books, 2011.

About the Author

Kene Iloenyosi (pronounced EELO-EN-YOSI) helps millennials discover and develop their talents, and then work in fulfilling careers. His first book, *Finding Your Sweet Spot*, has helped many start the talent discovery process. Kene works with corporations to maximize the talents of their millennial workforce. He is an author, speaker, and coach on talent-related topics, and the founder of Talent Revolution LLC, a company that develops talent discovery and development resources.

This book is Kene's way of sharing his personal struggle to find his Sweet Spot and grow in it. He and his wife Lucy live in Johns Creek, Georgia.